1960 U.K. YEARBOOK

ISBN: 9781695129030

This book gives a fascinating and informative insight into life in the United Kingdom in 1960. It includes everything from the most popular music of the year to the cost of a buying a new house. Additionally, there are chapters covering people in high office, the best-selling films of the year, and all the main news and events. Want to know which team won the FA Cup or which British personalities were born in 1960? All this and much more awaits you within.

FIRST EDITION

1960

January

M	T	W	T	F	S	S
				1	2	3
4	5	6	7	8	9	10
11	12	13	14	15	16	17
18	19	20	21	22	23	24
25	26	27	28	29	30	31

◐:5 ○:13 ◑:21 ●:28

February

M	T	W	T	F	S	S
1	2	3	4	5	6	7
8	9	10	11	12	13	14
15	16	17	18	19	20	21
22	23	24	25	26	27	28
29						

◐:4 ○:12 ◑:19 ●:26

March

M	T	W	T	F	S	S
	1	2	3	4	5	6
7	8	9	10	11	12	13
14	15	16	17	18	19	20
21	22	23	24	25	26	27
28	29	30	31			

◐:5 ○:13 ◑:20 ●:27

April

M	T	W	T	F	S	S
				1	2	3
4	5	6	7	8	9	10
11	12	13	14	15	16	17
18	19	20	21	22	23	24
25	26	27	28	29	30	

◐:4 ○:11 ◑:18 ●:25

May

M	T	W	T	F	S	S
						1
2	3	4	5	6	7	8
9	10	11	12	13	14	15
16	17	18	19	20	21	22
23	24	25	26	27	28	29
30	31					

◐:4 ○:11 ◑:17 ●:25

June

M	T	W	T	F	S	S
		1	2	3	4	5
6	7	8	9	10	11	12
13	14	15	16	17	18	19
20	21	22	23	24	25	26
27	28	29	30			

◐:2 ○:9 ◑:16 ●:24

July

M	T	W	T	F	S	S
				1	2	3
4	5	6	7	8	9	10
11	12	13	14	15	16	17
18	19	20	21	22	23	24
25	26	27	28	29	30	31

◐:2 ○:8 ◑:15 ●:23 ◐:31

August

M	T	W	T	F	S	S
1	2	3	4	5	6	7
8	9	10	11	12	13	14
15	16	17	18	19	20	21
22	23	24	25	26	27	28
29	30	31				

○:7 ◑:14 ●:22 ◐:29

September

M	T	W	T	F	S	S
			1	2	3	4
5	6	7	8	9	10	11
12	13	14	15	16	17	18
19	20	21	22	23	24	25
26	27	28	29	30		

○:5 ◑:12 ●:21 ◐:28

October

M	T	W	T	F	S	S
					1	2
3	4	5	6	7	8	9
10	11	12	13	14	15	16
17	18	19	20	21	22	23
24	25	26	27	28	29	30
31						

○:4 ◑:12 ●:20 ◐:27

November

M	T	W	T	F	S	S
	1	2	3	4	5	6
7	8	9	10	11	12	13
14	15	16	17	18	19	20
21	22	23	24	25	26	27
28	29	30				

○:3 ◑:11 ●:18 ◐:25

December

M	T	W	T	F	S	S
			1	2	3	4
5	6	7	8	9	10	11
12	13	14	15	16	17	18
19	20	21	22	23	24	25
26	27	28	29	30	31	

○:3 ◑:11 ●:18 ◐:25

PEOPLE IN HIGH OFFICE

Monarch - Queen Elizabeth II

Reign: 6th February 1952 - Present

Predecessor: King George VI

Heir Apparent: Charles, Prince of Wales

United Kingdom

Prime Minister
Harold Macmillan
Conservative Party
10th January 1957 - 19th October 1963

Australia

Canada

United States

Prime Minister
Sir Robert Menzies
19th December 1949 -
26th January 1966

Prime Minister
John Diefenbaker
21st June 1957 -
22nd April 1963

President
Dwight D. Eisenhower
20th January 1953 -
20th January 1961

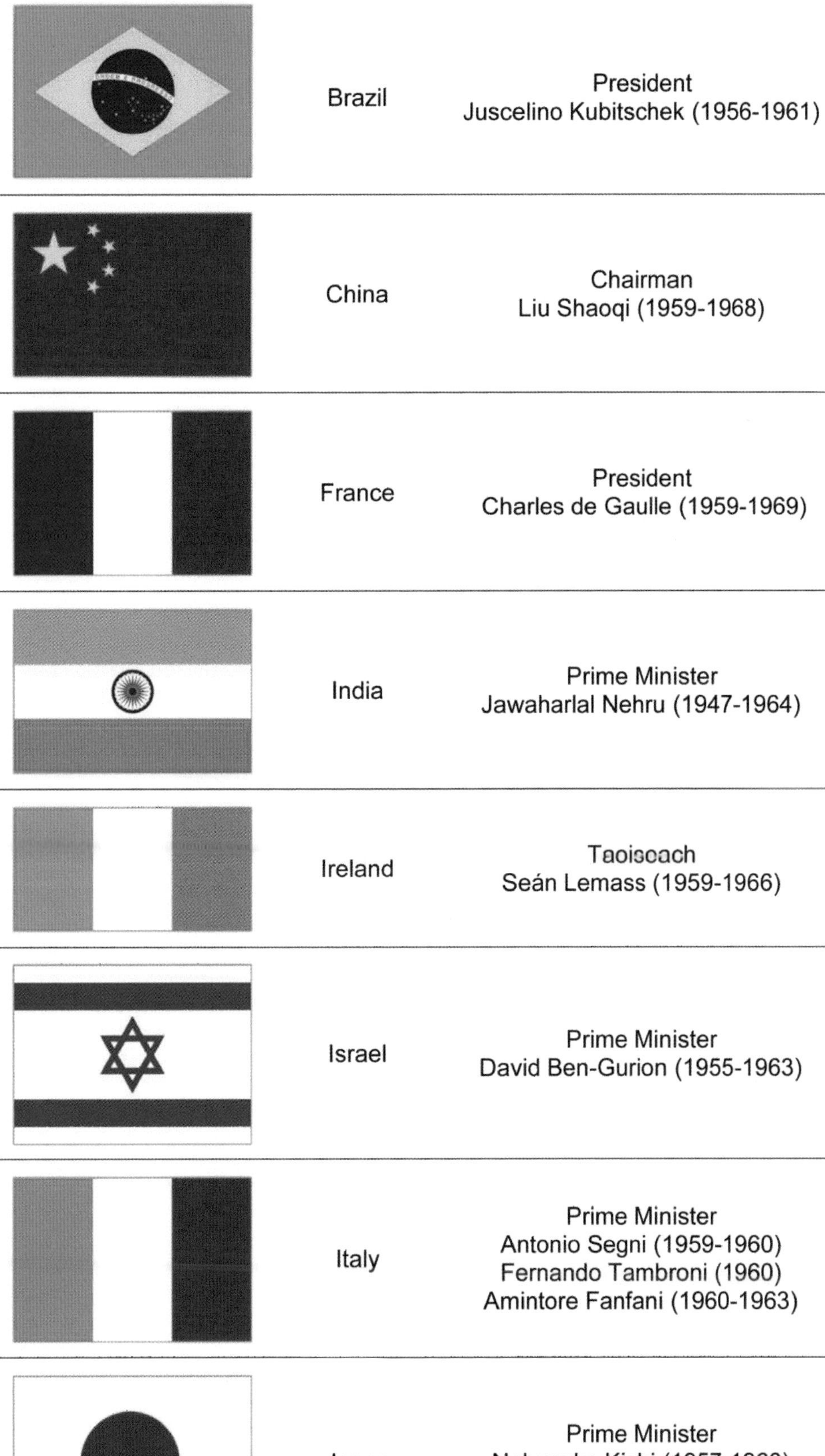

Brazil	President Juscelino Kubitschek (1956-1961)
China	Chairman Liu Shaoqi (1959-1968)
France	President Charles de Gaulle (1959-1969)
India	Prime Minister Jawaharlal Nehru (1947-1964)
Ireland	Taoiseach Seán Lemass (1959-1966)
Israel	Prime Minister David Ben-Gurion (1955-1963)
Italy	Prime Minister Antonio Segni (1959-1960) Fernando Tambroni (1960) Amintore Fanfani (1960-1963)
Japan	Prime Minister Nobusuke Kishi (1957-1960) Hayato Ikeda (1960-1964)

	Mexico	President Adolfo López Mateos (1958-1964)
	New Zealand	Prime Minister Walter Nash (1957-1960) Keith Holyoake (1960-1972)
	Pakistan	President Ayub Khan (1958-1969)
	South Africa	Prime Minister Hendrik Verwoerd (1958-1966)
	Soviet Union	Communist Party Leader Nikita Khrushchev (1953-1964)
	Spain	President Francisco Franco (1938-1973)
	Turkey	Prime Minister Adnan Menderes (1950-1960) Cemal Gürsel (1960-1961)
	West Germany	Chancellor Konrad Adenauer (1949-1963)

BRITISH NEWS & EVENTS

JAN

The state of emergency is lifted in Kenya officially signalling the end of the Mau Mau Uprising (1952-1960).

5th January: The Swansea and Mumbles Railway closes. The last train leaves Swansea for Mumbles at 11.52am (a ceremonial special carrying local dignitaries) and is driven by Frank Dukin, who had worked on the railway since 1907. *Fun facts: The Swansea and Mumbles Railway was the world's first passenger railway service. Originally built under an Act of Parliament of 1804 to move limestone from the quarries of Mumbles to Swansea, it carried the world's first fare-paying railway passengers in horse drawn carriages along the tramroad on the 25th March 1807. Pictured: Passengers board Car No.7 at Mumbles Pier Terminus (c. 1959).*

28th The final episode of comedy programme The Goon Show is broadcast by the BBC Home Service (now Radio 4). Starring Spike Milligan (the show's chief creator and main writer), Harry Secombe, Peter Sellers and Michael Bentine (series 1 and 2), it ran for 238 shows and 12 specials. *Fun facts: The first series, broadcast from the 28th May to 20th September 1951, was titled Crazy People; subsequent series had the title The Goon Show, inspired according to Spike Milligan by the Goons from Popeye.*

28th The comic ballet La fille mal gardée is premiered by The Royal Ballet at the Royal Opera House in London. Its popularity rapidly establishes it in the repertory of many ballet companies all over the world.

FEB

3rd | Prime Minister Harold Macmillan makes his famous 'Wind of Change' speech to the Parliament of South Africa. This historically significant address indicated a shift in British policy in regard to apartheid. *Note: The occasion was in fact the second time on which Macmillan had given this speech: he was repeating an address already made in Accra, Ghana (formerly the British colony of the Gold Coast) on the 10th January. This time though it received press attention, at least partly because of the stony reception that greeted it.*

8th | Queen Elizabeth II issues an Order-in-Council stating that the name Mountbatten-Windsor would be applied to male-line descendants of the Queen without royal styles and titles.

18th | Great Britain and Northern Ireland compete over 10 days at the Winter Olympics in Squaw Valley, California, United States, but do not win any medals.

19th | The Queen gives birth to her third child and second son. He is the first child born to a reigning British monarch since 1857.

MAR

Manchester City F.C. sign 20-year-old Scottish forward Denis Law for a national record fee of £55,000 from Huddersfield Town. *Fun facts: Law spent one year there before Torino bought him for £110,000, this time setting a new record fee for a transfer involving a British player. Although he played well in Italy, he found it difficult to settle there and signed for Manchester United in 1962, setting another British record transfer fee of £115,000. Law spent 11 years at Manchester United where he scored 237 goals in 404 appearances. He also played for Scotland a total of 55 times and jointly holds the Scottish international record goal tally (with Kenny Dalglish) of 30 goals.*

14th March - The Jodrell Bank Experimental Station at the University of Manchester (now the Jodrell Bank Observatory) makes contact with the American Pioneer 5 space probe over a record-breaking distance of 407,000 miles. *Follow up: Data was received from Pioneer 5 until the 30th April 1960, after which telemetry noise and weak signal strength made data reception impossible. Jodrell Bank last detected a signal from the spacecraft on the 26th June 1960, from a record distance of 22½ million miles. Pictured: The Lovell Telescope, used by Jodrell Bank to communicate with Pioneer 5, and the Pioneer 5 space probe.*

MAR

26th The Grand National horse race is televised for the first time with Peter O'Sullevan (who had covered the race on radio since 1947) commentating on his first of 37 televised Grand Nationals. The BBC's studio presenter, David Coleman, told viewers they were witnessing television history. The race was won by jockey Gerry Scott aboard 13/2 favourite Merryman II - the first clear favourite to win in 33 years.

28th A fire broke out in a bonded warehouse owned by Arbuckle, Smith and Company in Cheapside Street, Anderston, Glasgow. In total, 30 pumping appliances, five turntable ladders and four support vehicles were sent to the scene from around the area to tackle the blaze. The warehouse contained over a million gallons of whisky held in 21,000 wooden casks, and 30,000 gallons of rum. As the temperature of the fire increased some of these casks ruptured causing a massive boiling liquid expanding vapour explosion. This explosion burst the front and rear walls of the building outwards causing large quantities of masonry to collapse into the street. As a result of the collapse fourteen members of the Glasgow Fire Service and five members of the Glasgow Salvage Corps were killed.

31st The closing ceremony for the 18th century Naval dockyard at Sheerness on the Isle of Sheppey in Kent takes place. A total of 2,500 jobs have gradually been shed at the site since its closure was first announced by the government in February 1958.

APR

1st The first Dr. Martens (style 1460 boots) go on sale in the United Kingdom and are made by British shoe manufacturer R. Griggs Group Ltd. in their Cobbs Lane factory in Wollaston, Northamptonshire. *Fun facts: Today the footwear, distinguished by its air-cushioned 'AirWair' sole, sells in excess of 10 million pairs a year worldwide (only 1% of which are still made in the UK).*

8th The seven-week-old son of the Queen and the Duke of Edinburgh is christened Andrew Albert Christian Edward (he later becomes Prince Andrew, Duke of York).

13th The de Havilland Propellers 'Blue Streak', a British medium-range ballistic missile (MRBM), is cancelled without entering full production. The project was intended to maintain an independent British nuclear deterrent but it became clear that the missile system was too expensive and too vulnerable to a pre-emptive strike; the UK eventually purchased the Polaris submarine-launched ballistic missile system from the Americans.

17th American rock and roll singer Eddie Cochran, 21, dies 16 hours after a speeding taxi he was travelling in hits a lamppost going through Chippenham, Wiltshire. The taxi driver, Cochran's girlfriend Sharon Sheeley, tour manager Pat Thompkins, and singer Gene Vincent survived the crash, although Vincent sustained lasting injuries to an already damaged leg that would shorten his career and affect him for the rest of his life. Cochran's body was flown home to the United States and his remains were buried on the 25th April at Forest Lawn Memorial Park in Cypress, California.

18th At least 60,000 protesters gather at Trafalgar Square to mark the end of the third annual Aldermaston ban the bomb march, which had been organised by the Campaign for Nuclear Disarmament (CND).

APR

27th Harold Pinter's play The Caretaker premiers at the Arts Theatre Club in London's West End. It transfers to the Duchess Theatre the following month, where it runs for 444 performances before departing London for Broadway. The Caretaker remains one of Pinter's most celebrated and oft-performed plays.

30th Yorkshire County Cricket Club opens its first season since it was founded in 1883 under a professional captain, Vic Wilson. *Follow up: Wilson had a successful tenure at the club leading Yorkshire to the County Championship title in 1960 and 1962; he retired after the 1962 season and was succeeded by Brian Close.*

MAY

3rd Burnley F.C. win the Football League First Division title for the second time with a 2-1 win over Manchester City at Maine Road.

6th May - The Queens younger sister, Princess Margaret, marries photographer Antony Armstrong-Jones at Westminster Abbey in the first televised Royal marriage. Despite the public's enthusiasm for the wedding a number of critics were disapproving of a commoner marrying into the royal family. *Fun facts: 2,000 guests were invited for the wedding ceremony which attracted viewing figures in excess of 300 million worldwide. Following the wedding, as was the practice upon marriage into the Royal Family, Armstrong-Jones was granted a title and became the 1st Earl of Snowdon.*

18th The European Cup Final takes place at Glasgow's Hampden Park in front of 127,621 fans. The match sees the Spanish team Real Madrid beat German team Eintracht Frankfurt by 7 goals to 3 in what is widely regarded as one of the greatest football matches ever played.

JUN

24th June - The Avro 748 makes its maiden flight from the company's Woodford aircraft factory Cheshire. It goes into service the following year and is the last aircraft to be developed by Avro prior to its dissolution. *Fun facts: By 1988, the year in which production was terminated, 380 aircraft had been produced between Hawker Siddeley (the owning company of Avro) and Indian aviation company Hindustan Aeronautics Limited (HAL). Photo: A West Air Hawker Siddeley HS-748 Srs2 at Copenhagen Airport.*

26th — British Somaliland gains independence from the United Kingdom; five days later on the 1st July it unites with the former Italian Somaliland to create the Somali Republic.

28th — An explosion at the West District of the Old Coal Seam at Six Bells Colliery in Monmouthshire kills 45 out of the 48 men who were working in that part of the mine. A public enquiry into the disaster takes place at Newport Civic Centre between the 19th and 28th September 1960. The Inspector of Mines reports that the probable cause of the explosion was firedamp (flammable gas found in coal mines) ignited by a spark from a stone falling onto a steel girder.

JUL

The Shadows' instrumental Apache is released; it was recorded on the 17th June at the EMI Abbey Road Studio in London. *Fun facts: The tune topped the UK Singles Chart for five weeks and has been cited by a generation of guitarists as inspirational. It is considered one of the most influential British rock 45s of the pre-Beatle's era.*

14th — English primatologist Jane Goodall arrives at the Gombe Stream National Park in Tanganyika (present-day Tanzania) to begin her ground breaking behavioural study of chimpanzees in the wild. *Fun facts: Today Goodall is considered to be the world's foremost expert on chimpanzees and has received many honours for her environmental and humanitarian work. In April 2002 she was named a UN Messenger of Peace, and in 2004 was named a Dame Commander of the Most Excellent Order of the British Empire in an Investiture held in Buckingham Palace.*

JUL

21st Francis Chichester, English navigator and yachtsman, wins the first single-handed transatlantic yacht race. His arrival in New York aboard Gypsy Moth II after just 40 days also secures him a new record for a solo Atlantic crossing.

27th In a Cabinet reshuffle Selwyn Lloyd is appointed Chancellor of the Exchequer and Lord Home becomes Foreign Secretary.

30th The third Beaulieu Jazz Festival culminates in the so-called 'Battle of Beaulieu' as rival gangs of modern and traditional jazz fans clash.

AUG

7th The Bluebell Railway in Sussex begins regular operation as the first standard gauge steam-operated passenger heritage railway in the world.

16th Cyprus gains its independence from the United Kingdom; the Sovereign Base Areas of Akrotiri and Dhekelia remain as British Overseas Territories.

17th August - The Beatles, a five-strong male band from Liverpool (John Lennon, Paul McCartney, George Harrison, Stuart Sutcliffe and Pete Best), perform their first concert at the Indra Club in Hamburg, West Germany. *Fun facts: The Beatles regularly performed at different clubs in Hamburg during the period from August 1960 to December 1962; a chapter in the group's history which honed their performance skills, widened their reputation, and led to their first recording, My Bonnie. It was this record that brought them to the attention of Brian Epstein who became a key figure in their subsequent development and commercial success.*

22nd Beyond the Fringe, a British comedy stage revue written and performed by Peter Cook, Dudley Moore, Alan Bennett, and Jonathan Miller, premieres at the Royal Lyceum Theatre in Edinburgh. Hugely successful, it is widely regarded as seminal to the rise of satirical comedy in 1960s Britain.

SEP

The first Ten Tors Expedition takes place on Dartmoor with around 200 young people taking part.

10th In a deal worth £150,000 with the Football League to screen 26 matches, ITV broadcasts the first live Football League match to be shown on television. The game between Blackpool and Bolton Wanderers, at Bloomfield Road, kicked off at 6:50pm with live coverage starting at 7:30 under the title 'The Big Game'. A major blow to the TV moguls was the absence of big box-office draw Stanley Matthews through injury; the game ended 1-0 to Bolton in front of a half-empty stadium. *Follow up: ITV withdrew from the deal after the game when first Arsenal and then Tottenham Hotspur refused them permission to shoot at their matches. To see the next live game on British television you would have to wait 23 years until the 2nd October 1983; in that match Tottenham Hotspur beat Nottingham Forest 2-1 at White Hart Lane in front of 30,596 fans.*

15th September - The first traffic wardens are deployed in London after completing a fortnights training at Peel House, Regency Street, Pimlico. The 40 officers are sent off to sniff out the illegally parked Mini Coopers, Ford Anglia's and Morris Minors of Westminster and dish out fines of £2 apiece (around £46 in today's money). More than 300 tickets were issued on the day of introduction alone, totalling a tidy £600 for the Metropolitan Police. *Fun facts: The first ticket issued was to a Dr Thomas Creighton who had left his Ford Poplar at an angle outside a West End hotel. A newly-appointed warden, resplendent in his brass-buttoned uniform and yellow-banded hat, saw an opportunity and slapped on a ticket, unaware that Dr Creighton was in fact answering an emergency call to attend to a heart attack victim who had collapsed in the hotel. The ticket caused public outrage and the doctor's fine was subsequently waived.*

27th Europe's first 'moving pavement' (the Trav-O-Lator), opens at Bank station on the London Underground.

SEP

29th	'Tell Laura I Love Her' by Welsh singer Ricky Valance (born David Spencer) peaks at No.1 in UK. The record sells over a million copies and Valance becomes the first Welshman to top the British singles chart (Shirley Bassey was the first Welsh female with 'As I Love You' in February 1959).

OCT

1st	Nigeria gains its independence from the United Kingdom; six days later it becomes the 99th member of the United Nations.
5th	Against the wishes of leader Hugh Gaitskell, the Labour party votes in favour of unilateral nuclear disarmament by Britain at its Scarborough conference. Although Gaitskell loses the vote, the decision is reversed the following year.
7th	Severe flooding occurs in Horncastle, Lincolnshire, resulting in a UK weather record 178mm total rainfall over 180-minutes.
8th	The Sheffield Tramway closes with the last trams running between Leopold Street to Beauchief and Tinsley - this left Blackpool as the only place in England with electric trams. *Fun facts: 34 years later trams returned to the streets of Sheffield under a new network called the Sheffield Supertram.*
17th	The News Chronicle ceases publication and is absorbed into the Daily Mail.

21st October (Trafalgar Day) - The Queen launches Britain's first nuclear submarine, HMS Dreadnought (S101). Built by Vickers Armstrongs at Barrow-in-Furness, Cumbria, it is the seventh naval vessel to bear the name Dreadnought. The submarine is powered by a S5W reactor, a design made available as a direct result of the 1958 US-UK Mutual Defence Agreement. *Follow up: During her career Dreadnought performed many varied missions including, in 1971, becoming the first British submarine to surface at the North Pole. Dreadnought was withdrawn from service in 1980.*

OCT

25th | Two barges (named the Arkendale H and Wastdale H) collide with one of the columns of the Severn Railway Bridge in heavy fog, causing two spans of the twenty-two-span steel and cast-iron bridge to collapse. It is never repaired and in August 1967 British Rail award the contract to demolish the bridge to Nordman Construction.

27th October - Severe flooding occurs in the valley of the River Exe and surrounding areas of Devon following heavy rainfall. The Exe overflows from above Exwick down through St Thomas and towards the low-lying parts of Alphington. The water rises as high as 2m above ground level and 150 employees of the local firm Beach Bros become trapped for nine hours; in total 2,500 properties are flooded. *Follow up: These floods led to the construction of new flood defences for Exeter. Work began in 1965, took 12 years to complete and cost £8 million.*

27th | The film Saturday Night and Sunday Morning is released. It is one of a series of 'kitchen sink drama' films made in the late 1950s and early 1960s, and is part of the British New Wave of filmmaking. In 1999 the British Film Institute named Saturday Night and Sunday Morning the 14th greatest film of all time on their Top 100 British films list.

30th | The first kidney transplant in the UK is performed by surgeon Michael Woodruff (between identical twins) at the Royal Infirmary in Edinburgh.

NOV

2nd | Penguin Books is found not guilty of obscenity for publishing D. H. Lawrence's novel Lady Chatterley's Lover; it quickly goes on to sell 3 million copies.

NOV

4th | At the Kasakela Chimpanzee Community, Jane Goodall observes a chimpanzee (named David Greybeard) using a grass stalk to extract termites from a termite hill. It is the first recorded case of tool use by animals.

4th | British paleoanthropologist Mary Leakey and husband Louis Leakey discover the first Homo habilis jaw fragments (OH 7) at Olduvai Gorge in Tanzania.

DEC

1st | Beatles Paul McCartney and Pete Best are arrested in Hamburg. They are accused of attempted arson by Kaiserkeller club owner Bruno Koschmider after their contract to play at his club was terminated. McCartney and Best spend the night in jail before being released. They are deported from Germany the following day.

2nd | The Archbishop of Canterbury, Geoffrey Fisher, meets with Pope John XXIII in the Vatican. It is the first time an Archbishop of Canterbury has visited the Vatican for 600 years.

9th December - The first episode of the soap opera Coronation Street, made by Granada Television in Manchester, is aired on ITV. Characters introduced in the first episode include Ken Barlow (William Roache), Ena Sharples (Violet Carson), Elsie Tanner (Pat Phoenix) and Annie Walker (Doris Speed). *Fun facts: In September 2010 Coronation Street became the world's longest-running television soap opera and was listed in Guinness World Records. Photo: The cast of Coronation Street in the Granada TV Centre car park between rehearsals for the first programme.*

10th | Brazilian-born British biologist Sir Peter Brian Medawar and Australian Sir Frank Macfarlane Burnet win the Nobel Prize in Physiology or Medicine 'for discovery of acquired immunological tolerance'.

31st | The farthing, first minted in 1860, ceases to become legal tender.

31st | Call-ups for National Service formally end (the last National Servicemen left the armed forces in May 1963).

50 Worldwide News & Events

1. 1st January - The Bank of France issues the 'new franc', worth 100 times the value of existing francs.
2. 2nd January - The U.S. Senator for Massachusetts, John F. Kennedy, announces his candidacy for the Democratic presidential nomination to replace incumbent President Dwight D. Eisenhower.
3. 20th January - At Tank Range 42 in Grafenwoehr, West Germany, Elvis Presley is promoted to the rank of sergeant.
4. 23rd January - Swiss oceanographer Jacques Piccard and American Navy Lieutenant Don Walsh descend into the Challenger Deep in the Mariana Trench near Guam in the Pacific. The crew of two, aboard the deep-diving research bathyscaphe Trieste, reach a record maximum depth of 35,797ft (10,911m) in the deepest known part of the Earth's ocean.

5. 1st February - In Greensboro, North Carolina, four black students from North Carolina Agricultural and Technical State University begin a sit-in at a segregated Woolworth's lunch counter. Whilst the Greensboro sit-ins are not the first sit-ins of the American Civil Rights Movement, they become the most well-known and lead to increased national sentiment at a crucial period in U.S. history. *Photo: The Greensboro 4 - David Richmond, Franklin McCain, Ezell Blair, Jr., and Joseph McNeil.*

6. 3rd February - La Dolce Vita, directed by Federico Fellini and starring Marcello Mastroianni and Anita Ekberg, has its film premiere in Rome, Italy. *Fun facts: The film became a massive box office hit in Europe and was the winner of the Palme d'Or at the 1960 Cannes Film Festival.*

7. 13th February - France performs its first nuclear test, code-named Gerboise Bleue (Blue Desert Rat), at the Reganne Oasis in the Sahara Desert of Algeria. With an explosive yield of 65 kilotons, Gerboise Bleue was relatively large for a country's first nuclear test, around four times more powerful than the atomic bomb dropped on Hiroshima in 1945.
8. 29th February - An earthquake near the city of Agadir in Morocco kills a third of the population of the city (between 12,000 and 15,000 people). In addition to the deaths another 12,000 are injured, and at least 35,000 people are left homeless, in what is the most destructive and deadliest earthquake in Moroccan history.

9. 2nd March - Elvis Presley says goodbye to fans and media as he departs West Germany to fly home to the U.S. The next day at 7:42am his plane arrives at McGuire Air Force Base near Fort Dix, New Jersey. Nancy Sinatra, RCA representatives, manager Colonel Tom Parker, and a huge crowd of fans are there to welcome him home. Two days later, on the 5th March, Presley is officially discharged from active duty after his 2-year stint in Army. *Fun fact: En route home Presley's plane stopped at Prestwick Airport in Scotland to refuel; this is the one and only documented time that he set foot in the United Kingdom.*

10. 4th March - The French freighter La Coubre explodes in the harbour of Havana, Cuba, whilst unloading 76 tons of grenades and munitions. Around 100 people are believed to have been killed and many more are injured. Cuban Prime Minister Fidel Castro charged it was an act of sabotage on the part of the United States, which denied any involvement.
11. 18th March - The fifth edition of the annual Eurovision Song Contest takes place at the Royal Festival Hall in London. The winner is 18-year-old Jacqueline Boyer from France singing Tom Pillibi.
12. 21st March - Sharpeville Massacre: After a day of demonstrations against pass laws a crowd of around 6,000 protesters converge on a police station in the township of Sharpeville in Transvaal. The South African police open fire on the crowd killing 69 and injuring 180 others - many are shot in the back as they flee.

13. 22nd March - American physicists Arthur Leonard Schawlow and Charles Hard Townes receive the first patent for a laser.
14. 28th March - Pope John XXIII appoints the first Japanese, African and Filipino cardinals of the modern era (Laurean Rugambwa, Peter Doi and Rufino Santos).
15. 1st April - The U.S. launches the first successful low-Earth orbital weather satellite TIROS-1 from Cape Canaveral, Florida.

16. 4th April - The 32nd Academy Awards ceremony, to honour the best in film from 1959, takes place at the RKO Pantages Theatre in Hollywood. Hosted by Bob Hope, the winners include director William Wyler, Charlton Heston, Simone Signoret, Hugh Griffith and Shelley Winters. The epic drama Ben-Hur wins 11 Oscars (including Best Motion Picture) breaking the record of nine set the previous year by Gigi.

17. 13th April - Transit 1B is launched from Cape Canaveral, Florida, and becomes the first navigational satellite to be placed in orbit around Earth.
18. 14th April - The record company Motown, originally founded by Berry Gordy Jr. as Tamla Records on the 12th January 1959, is incorporated as Motown Record Corporation.
19. 21st April - Brasilia is founded and replaces Rio de Janeiro as the new national capital of Brazil.
20. 24th April - The 14th Annual Tony Awards take place at the Astor Hotel Grand Ballroom in New York City. In front of 1,200 attendees Michael Kidd receives his fifth Tony Award for choreography, Mary Martin wins her third award as an actress in a musical, and the best musical award sees a tie between Fiorello! and The Sound of Music.
21. 25th April - The American nuclear submarine USS Triton, under the command of Captain Edward L. Beach, Jr., completes the first underwater circumnavigation of the Earth.

22. 3rd May - The Anne Frank House, a writer's house and biographical museum dedicated to Jewish wartime diarist Anne Frank, opens in Amsterdam, Netherlands.

23. 11th May - In Buenos Aires, Argentina, Israeli soldiers launch a successful and audacious operation to abduct Nazi war criminal Adolf Eichmann and fly him to Israel to stand trial. *Follow up: Eichmann, one of the primary organisers of the Holocaust, went on trial on the 11th April 1961. He was found guilty and sentenced to death by hanging on the 1st June 1962.*

24. 12th May - The American television station ABC broadcasts The Frank Sinatra Timex Special featuring Elvis Presley in his first televised appearance following his military service in West Germany. During the show Presley sings a number of songs and also performs together with Sinatra; they each sing a song that other had made famous and take turns to sing each verse - Presley sings Witchcraft and Sinatra sings Love Me Tender.

25. 22nd May - Valdivia earthquake: Chile's subduction fault ruptures from Talcahuano to the Taitao Peninsula (with its epicenter near Lumaco), causing the most powerful earthquake on record (with a magnitude of 9.5) and a tsunami. The tsunami affects southern Chile, Hawaii, Japan, the Philippines, eastern New Zealand, southeast Australia, and the Aleutian Islands. The death toll arising from this widespread disaster is not certain - various estimates of the total number of fatalities range between 1,000 and 7,000.

26. 20th June - At the Polo Grounds in New York City, Floyd Patterson knocks-out Ingemar Johansson in the fifth round to become the first man in history to regain the undisputed World Heavyweight Championship. *Fun facts: As an amateur Patterson won a gold medal in the middleweight division at the 1952 Summer Olympics, and in 1956, at the age of 21, became the youngest boxer in history to win the world heavyweight championship title. Patterson retired from boxing after losing to Muhammad Ali in September 1972, and was inducted into the International Boxing Hall of Fame in 1991.*

27. 26th June - Madagascar gains full independence from France.

28. July - An 18-year-old Chubby Checker performs 'The Twist' for the first time in front of a live audience at the Rainbow Club in Wildwood, New Jersey. *Fun facts: The Twist reaches the No.1 spot on the Billboard Hot 100 on the 19th September and quickly becomes responsible for a dance craze that would sweep the Western world during the early 1960s.*

29. 6th July - Russian-born British engineer Dr Barbara Moore becomes the first woman to complete the 3,387-mile walk from San Francisco to New York City. A vegetarian and a breatharian, Moore undertook the 86-day marathon walk with only nuts, honey, raw fruit and vegetable juice for nourishment.

30. 11th July - Harper Lee releases her critically acclaimed novel To Kill a Mockingbird. *Fun facts: The 1961 Pulitzer Prize winning novel became an instant success and has become a classic of modern American literature. It was Lee's only published book until Go Set a Watchman, an early draft of To Kill a Mockingbird, was published in July 2015.*

31. 21st July - Sirimavo Bandaranaike becomes the world's first non-hereditary female head of government in modern history when she is elected Prime Minister of Ceylon (now Sri Lanka). *Fun fact: Bandaranaike served three terms as Prime Minister: 1960-1965, 1970-1977 and 1994-2000.*

32. 6th August - The Cuban government, under President Osvaldo Dorticós Torrado and Prime Minister Fidel Castro, nationalises all American owned oil refineries located within Cuba's national borders (approximately $1.7 billion in oil assets which, when adjusted for inflation, amounts to $14.7 billion as of 2019).

33. 10th August - Discoverer 13, a strategic reconnaissance satellite produced and operated by the CIA Directorate of Science & Technology and the U.S. Air Force, is launched into orbit. *Fun facts: The return capsule of the Discoverer 13 was successfully recovered the next day; this was the first man-made object ever recovered of a from space beating the Soviet Korabl-Sputnik 2 by nine days.*

34. 14th August - Australian driver Jack Brabham clinches the Formula 1 World Drivers Championship by winning the Portuguese Grand Prix at Boavista. *Fun facts: This was Brabham's second World Championship win having previously won it a year earlier in 1959. He would go on to win a third and final title in 1966. Photo: Brabham leading the 1960 Grand Prix of Portugal in his Cooper-Climax T53.*

35. 16th August - U.S. Air Force Captain Joseph Kittinger parachutes from a balloon over New Mexico at 102,800 feet (31,333 meters). Kittinger falls for 4 minutes and 36 seconds, reaching a maximum speed of 614 miles per hour (988 km/h) before opening his parachute at 18,000 feet; his jump set records for highest balloon ascent, highest parachute jump, longest-duration drogue-fall, and fastest speed by a human being through the atmosphere.

36. 19th August - The Soviet artificial satellite Korabl-Sputnik 2 (also known as Sputnik 5 in the West) is launched into orbit. The spacecraft, carrying two dogs, Belka and Strelka, 40 mice, two rats and a variety of plants, is the first to send animals into orbit and return them safely back to Earth; the flight paved the way for the first human orbital flight, Vostok 1, which was launched less than eight months later. *Fun fact: Spacedog Strelka had a litter of puppies a year after the flight, one of which, Pushinka, was given to American First Lady Jacqueline Kennedy as a goodwill present from the Soviet Union.*

37. 23rd August - The world's largest frog, a goliath frog weighing 3.3kg, is caught in Equatorial Guinea.

38. 24th August - The coldest ever temperature recorded on Earth is measured at -88.3°C (-126.9°F) at Vostok, Antarctica. *Fun fact: The current record (also at Vostok) stands at -89.2 °C (-128.6 °F), recorded on the 21st July 1983.*

39. 25th August - The 17th Summer Olympic Games open in Rome, Italy.

40. 5th September - 18-year-old Cassius Clay beats 3-time European champion Zbigniew Pietrzykowski of Poland, by a unanimous points decision, to win Olympic light heavyweight boxing gold medal. *Fun facts: Cassius Clay changed his name to Muhammad Ali on the 6th March 1964 after converting to Islam. He defeated every top heavyweight in his era and was named Fighter of the Year by The Ring magazine more times than any other fighter. He was nicknamed 'The Greatest' and is widely regarded as one of the most significant and celebrated sports figures of the 20th century, and as one of the greatest boxers of all time. Ali was inducted into the International Boxing Hall of Fame in 1990.*

41. 20th September - The United Nations General Assembly admits 13 African nations, and Cyprus, to bring the total number of member states to 96.
42. 30th September - Hanna-Barbera's show The Flintstones premieres on the U.S. network TV station ABC and becomes televisions first animated sitcom. *Fun facts: The Flintstones was the most financially successful (and longest-running) network animated franchise for three decades, until The Simpsons debuted in late 1989. In 2013, TV Guide ranked The Flintstones the second-greatest TV cartoon of all time (after The Simpsons).*
43. 10th October - A severe cyclonic storm ravages East-Pakistan. Entire villages are wiped out by the storm and approximately 35,000 homes are destroyed (most of which were thatched huts made of bamboo and mud). The worst damage takes place on Ramgati Island where 3,500 people are killed; roughly 95 percent of the island's structure is destroyed forcing residents to cling to trees for survival. In total an estimated 6,000 people perish as a result the Cyclone and 100,000 are left homeless.
44. 11th October - The 11th General Conference on Weights and Measures establishes the International System of Units (abbreviated SI from the French name 'Le Système international d'unités').

45. 29th October - Cassius Clay wins his first professional fight after 6 rounds with a unanimous decision against Tunney Hunsaker in Louisville, Kentucky. After the fight Hunsaker said, "Clay was as fast as lightning ... I tried every trick I knew to throw at him off balance but he was just too good".

46. 8th November - U.S. Presidential election: In a closely contested election, Democrat John F. Kennedy defeats incumbent Vice President Richard Nixon, the Republican Party nominee, to become the youngest person (at 43) to be elected president. *Fun facts: Kennedy won a 303 to 219 Electoral College victory and is generally considered to have won the national popular vote by 112,827, a margin of just 0.17 percent. This was the first election in which all fifty states participated, and was also the first election in which an incumbent president was ineligible to run for a third term due to the term limits established by the 22nd Amendment. Photo: Senator Kennedy with his wife Jacqueline and daughter Caroline outside their home in Hyannis Port, Massachusetts on the 8th November 1960.*

47. 13th November - A fire at a cinema in Amûde, Syria kills over 180 children.
48. 28th November - Mauritania gains its independence from France.
49. 10th December - American physical chemist Willard Libby wins the Nobel prize in Chemistry for his work developing carbon-14 dating (radiocarbon dating).
50. 28th December - In the 49th Davis Cup Australia beats Italy 4-1 at White City Stadium in Sydney, Australia. *Fun facts: It was Italy's first appearance in a Davis Cup final, and it was the first final not to feature the United States since 1936.*

Births

U.K. Personalities

Born in 1960

Nigella Lucy Lawson
b. 6th January 1960

Food writer and cooking show host. After graduating from Oxford University Lawson started work as a book reviewer and restaurant critic, later becoming the deputy literary editor of The Sunday Times. In 1998 her first cookery book, How to Eat, was published and sold 300,000 copies - she has since won a number of awards and has sold more than 3 million cookery books worldwide. On television Lawson has been a regular host of cooking shows since 1999.

Prince Andrew, Duke of York, KG, GCVO, CD, ADC(P)
b. 19th February 1960

The third child and second son of Queen Elizabeth II and Prince Philip, Duke of Edinburgh. At the time of his birth he was second in the line of succession to the British throne; as of May 2019, he is eighth in line. He holds the rank of commander and the honorary rank of Vice Admiral in the Royal Navy (in which he saw active service during the Falklands War). As well as carrying out his official engagements Prince Andrew served as Britain's Special Representative for International Trade and Investment from 2001 until 2011.

Jenny Éclair
b. 16th March 1960

Comedian, novelist and actress who was born Jenny Clare Hargreaves to English parents in Kuala Lumpur, Malaysia. Eclair's first job was at Camberwell Arts College as a life model before she saw an advert in The Stage looking for novelty acts and found work doing punk poems. In 1995 she became the first female solo winner of the Edinburgh Fringe Festival's Perrier Comedy Award. She is probably best known today for her roles in Grumpy Old Women (2004-2007) and in Loose Women (2011-2012).

Linford Cicero Christie, OBE
b. 2nd April 1960

Jamaican-born former sprinter who is the only British man to have won gold medals in the 100 metres at all four major competitions open to British athletes; the World Championships, the European Championships, the Commonwealth Games and the Olympic Games (at 32-years-old he remains the oldest male athlete to win the 100m at an Olympic Games). Christie was the first European to break the 10-second barrier in the 100m and still holds the British record in the event with a time of 9.87s.

Jeremy Charles Robert Clarkson
b. 11th April 1960

Broadcaster, journalist and writer who is best known for co-presenting the BBC TV show Top Gear with Richard Hammond and James May from October 2002 to March 2015. Since leaving the BBC Clarkson has co-produced and starred in The Grand Tour for Amazon Video, and has become the new host of Who Wants to Be a Millionaire? for ITV. He has also written books on subjects such as history and engineering, as well as writing weekly columns for The Sunday Times and The Sun.

Gary Rhodes, OBE
b. 22nd April 1960

Restaurateur and television chef known for his love of British cuisine, and the distinctive spiked hair style that he once wore. He has fronted shows such as MasterChef, MasterChef USA, Hell's Kitchen, and his own series Rhodes Around Britain, as well as featuring in ITV's Saturday Cooks programme and the UKTV Food show Local Food Hero. Additionally, Rhodes owns four restaurants and has his own line of cookware and bread mixes. He was created an OBE in June 2006.

Dame Kristin Ann Scott Thomas, DBE
b. 24th May 1960

Actress who is a five-time BAFTA Award nominee, winning once for Best Actress in a Supporting Role for Four Weddings and a Funeral (1994), and a five-times Olivier Award nominee, winning once for Best Actress in 2008 for the Royal Court revival of The Seagull. She has also been nominated for the Academy Award for Best Actress for The English Patient (1996). Scott Thomas was made a Dame Commander of the Order of the British Empire (DBE) in the 2015 New Year Honours for her services to drama.

Shaun Anthony Linford Wallace
b. 2nd June 1960

English barrister, lecturer and television personality of Jamaican descent. Wallace is best known as a 'Chaser' on the ITV quiz show The Chase. He is also a part-time lecturer and often visits schools, colleges and other institutions to educate students on the many aspects of law. In 2004 Wallace won the BBC television game show Mastermind, and in 2008 was a finalist on the first series of the quiz show Are You an Egghead?, narrowly losing out to Barry Simmons.

Bradley John Walsh
b. 4th June 1960

Actor, comedian, singer, television presenter and former professional footballer who first came to prominence on television in 1994 after he won a role as one of the presenting team on the National Lottery on BBC One. He has been a regular on British television screens since and is known for his roles as Danny Baldwin in Coronation Street, DS Ronnie Brooks in Law & Order: UK, Graham O'Brien in Doctor Who, and for hosting ITV game shows The Chase, and Cash Trapped.

Michael James Hucknall
b. 8th June 1960

Music artist who achieved international fame in the 1980s as the lead singer and songwriter of the soul-influenced pop band Simply Red, with whom he enjoyed a 25-year career and sold over 50 million albums. Since the release of Simply Red's debut studio album Picture Book (1985), they have had ten songs reach top 10 in the U.K Singles Chart, and have had five No.1 albums; their 1991 album, Stars, has been certified twelve times platinum and is one of the best-selling albums in U.K. chart history.

Jack Wilson McConnell, Baron McConnell of Glenscorrodale, PC
b. 30th June 1960

Scottish politician and a Labour life peer in the House of Lords who was the First Minister of Scotland from 2001 to 2007, and was the Member of the Scottish Parliament for Motherwell and Wishaw from 1999 to 2011. Three years after losing office as First Minister of Scotland McConnell became a member of the House of Lords and made a commitment to continuing his work to tackle poverty in Africa and to develop the relationship between Scotland and Malawi.

Vince Clarke
b. 3rd July 1960

Synthpop musician and songwriter born Vincent John Martin. Clarke has been the main composer and musician of the band Erasure since its inception in 1985, and was previously the main songwriter for several groups, including Depeche Mode, Yazoo, and The Assembly. As part of Erasure, with singer Andy Bell, the duo has seen 34 of their 37 chart-eligible singles and EPs make the U.K. Top 40. They have also sold over 25 million albums worldwide and were the winners of the Brit Award for Best British Group in 1989.

Caroline Quentin
b. 11th July 1960

Actress, born Caroline Jones, who has become known for her television appearances in programs such as Men Behaving Badly (1992-1998), Jonathan Creek (1997-2000), Blue Murder (2003-2009), Life Begins (2004-2006), and since 2017, The World's Most Extraordinary Homes. Quentin has coeliac disease and is the current patron of Coeliac U.K. She is also the current president of the charity Campaign for National Parks, promoting the National Parks of England and Wales.

Ian David Hislop
b. 13th July 1960

Journalist, satirist, writer, broadcaster, and editor of the magazine Private Eye. He has appeared on many radio and television programmes and has been a team captain on the BBC quiz show Have I Got News for You since the programme's inception in 1990. In 2003 he was listed in The Observer as one of the 50 funniest acts in British comedy. Hislop also has a career as an after-dinner speaker and awards presenter, working for several speaker bureaux.

Philip Douglas Taylor
b. 13th August 1960

Retired professional darts player nicknamed The Power. He is widely regarded as the greatest darts player of all time having won 214 professional tournaments, including 85 major titles and a record 16 World Championships. He won eight consecutive World Championships from 1995 to 2002, and reached 14 consecutive finals from 1994 to 2007 (both records). He was also the first person to hit two nine-dart finishes in one match, and has hit a record 11 televised nine-dart finishes.

Sarah Brightman
b. 14th August 1960

Classical crossover soprano, singer, songwriter, actress, dancer and musician. Brightman began her career as a member of the dance troupe Hot Gossip, and in 1981 made her West End debut in Cats. She has since starred in several West End and Broadway musicals including Phantom of The Opera (from which a CD released in 1987 sold 40 million copies worldwide). Brightman has sung in many languages throughout her career and has collected over 200 gold and platinum record awards from 38 different countries.

Shirley Annette Ballas
b. 8th September 1960

Ballroom dancer, dance teacher, and dance adjudicator who specialises in the International Latin division, where she won several championship titles which earned her the nickname The Queen of Latin. Ballas stopped competing in dance competitions in 1996, becoming a dance coach and judge for ballroom and Latin American competitions. In 2017 she was appointed head judge on the BBC TV show Strictly Come Dancing following the departure of Len Goodman.

Hugh John Mungo Grant
b. 9th September 1960

Actor and film producer who achieved international success after appearing in Four Weddings and a Funeral (1994). His success continued with performances in films such as Mickey Blue Eyes (1999), Notting Hill (1999), and Bridget Jones's Diary (2001). Most recently he has received critical acclaim for his turns as Phoenix Buchanan in Paddington 2 (2017), and as Jeremy Thorpe in the BBC miniseries A Very English Scandal (2018). As of 2018 his films have grossed nearly US$3 billion worldwide.

Colin Andrew Firth, CBE
b. 10th September 1960

Actor who has received an Academy Award, a Golden Globe Award, two BAFTA Awards and three Screen Actors Guild Awards. Firth first received widespread attention for his portrayal of Fitzwilliam Darcy in the 1995 television adaptation of Jane Austen's Pride and Prejudice. This led to roles in films such as The English Patient (1996), Bridget Jones's Diary (2001) and Kingsman (2014). Firth won the Academy Award for Best Actor in 2010 playing King George VI in Tom Hooper's The King's Speech.

Damon Graham Devereux Hill, OBE
b. 17th September 1960

Former racing driver who started his career on motorbikes in 1981 and after minor success moved on to single-seater racing cars. Hill became a test driver for the Formula One title-winning Williams team in 1992, and was promoted to the Williams race team the following year. He took the first of his 22 Formula One victories at the 1993 Hungarian Grand Prix and became champion in 1996 with eight wins. Hill retired from racing after the 1999 season and currently works as part of the Sky Sports F1 broadcasting team.

Jonathan Stephen Ross, OBE
b. 17th November 1960

Television and radio presenter, film critic, actor, and comedian best known for presenting the BBC One chat show Friday Night with Jonathan Ross during the 2000s (for which he won three BAFTA awards; 2004, 2006 and 2007). Ross has been a regular on British television screens since 1987 and has also hosted his own radio show on BBC Radio 2. Since leaving the BBC in 2010 he has been the host of The Jonathan Ross Show on ITV. Ross was made an OBE for his services to broadcasting in 2005.

Kim Wilde
b. 18th November 1960

Pop singer, author, DJ and television presenter who burst onto the music scene in 1981 with her debut single 'Kids in America'. Between 1981 and 1996 she had 25 singles reach the Top 50 in the U.K. and holds the record for being the most-charted British female solo act of the 1980s. In 1998, while still active in music, Wilde branched into a new career as a landscape gardener which has included presenting gardening shows on the BBC and Channel 4.

John Charles Galliano, CBE, RDI
b. 28th November 1960

Gibraltar-born British fashion designer, born Juan Carlos Antonio Galliano-Guillén, who was the head designer of French fashion companies Givenchy (1995-1996), Christian Dior (1996-2011), and his own label John Galliano (1988-2011). Since 2014 he has been the creative director of Paris-based fashion house Maison Margiela. Galliano has won the British Designer of the Year four times (1987, 1994, 1995, 1997), and in a 2004 poll for the BBC he was named the fifth most influential person in British culture.

Gary Winston Lineker, OBE
b. 30th November 1960

Former professional footballer who began his career at Leicester City in 1978 and went on to play for Everton, Barcelona, Tottenham Hotspur and Nagoya Grampus Eight. He made his England debut in 1984, earning 80 caps and scoring 48 goals. During his 16-year career Lineker never received a yellow or red card and as a result he was honoured in 1990 with the FIFA Fair Play Award. Since the late 1990s Lineker has presented the BBC's flagship football programme Match of the Day.

Sir Kenneth Charles Branagh
b. 10th December 1960

Northern Irish actor, director, producer, and screenwriter. Branagh trained at the Royal Academy of Dramatic Art in London, and in 2015 succeeded Richard Attenborough as its president. He has both directed and starred in several film adaptations of William Shakespeare's plays. Branagh has starred in numerous other films and television series, won three BAFTAs, and an Emmy Award. He was appointed a Knight Bachelor in the 2012 Birthday Honours and was made a Freeman of his native city of Belfast in January 2018.

Christopher Roland Waddle
b. 14th December 1960

Former professional football player and manager who currently works as a commentator and pundit. During his professional career, which lasted from 1978 to 1998, he played as a midfielder for several clubs including Newcastle United, Tottenham Hotspur, Sheffield Wednesday, and Olympique de Marseille in France. Waddle earned 62 caps for the England national football team between 1985 and 1991, and was a member of the England squads for the 1986 & 1990 World Cups, and Euro 1988.

Carol Jean Vorderman, MBE
b. 24th December 1960

Media personality best known for co-hosting the popular game show Countdown (1982-2008) and for being a presenter on ITV's Loose Women (2011-2014). She has also had newspaper columns in The Daily Telegraph and Daily Mirror, written books on subjects ranging from school textbooks on mathematics to a No.1 best-selling book on Detox diets, and has hosted the Pride of Britain awards since 1999 to honour British people who have acted bravely or extraordinarily in challenging situations.

Noteable British Deaths

7th Jan	Dorothea Lambert Chambers (née Dorothea Katherine Douglass, 3rd September 1878) - Tennis player who won seven Wimbledon Women's Singles titles and a gold medal at the 1908 Summer Olympics.
9th Jan	Elsie Jeanette Dunkerley (b. 25th November 1880) - Girls' story writer who took the name Oxenham as her pseudonym when her first book, Goblin Island, was published in 1907. In her lifetime she had 87 titles published; her Abbey Series of 38 books are her best-known and best-loved.
11th Jan	Lady Isabel Galloway Emslie Hutton, CBE (née Isabel Galloway Emslie, 1887) - Scottish medical doctor specialising in mental health and social work who was awarded the Serbian orders of the White Eagle and St. Sava, the French Croix de Guerre, and the Order of St. Anna of Russia.
12th Jan	Nevil Shute Norway (b. 17th January 1899) - Novelist and aeronautical engineer who spent his later years in Australia. Norway's novels were written under the pen name Nevil Shute and include A Town Like Alice (1950), and On the Beach (1957).
25th Jan	Rutland Boughton (b. 23rd January 1878) - Composer of opera and choral music. In addition to his compositions Boughton is remembered for his attempt to create an 'English Bayreuth' at Glastonbury, establishing the first series of Glastonbury Festivals which ran with enormous success from 1914 until 1926.
8th Feb	John Langshaw Austin (b. 26th March 1911) - Philosopher of language and leading proponent of ordinary language philosophy, perhaps best known for developing the theory of speech acts.
8th Feb	Sir Giles Gilbert Scott, OM, RA (b. 9th November 1880) - Architect noted for his blending of Gothic tradition with modernism and for his work on the Cambridge University Library, Oxford's Lady Margaret Hall, Battersea Power Station and Liverpool Cathedral. Scott also designed the iconic red telephone box.
20th Feb	Sir Charles Leonard Woolley (b. 17th April 1880) - Archaeologist best known for his excavations at Ur in Mesopotamia. He is recognised as one of the first 'modern' archaeologists, excavating in a methodical way and keeping careful records to reconstruct ancient life and history.
21st Feb	Edwina Cynthia Annette Mountbatten, Countess Mountbatten of Burma, CI, GBE, DCVO, GCStJ (née Ashley, 28th November 1900) - Heiress, socialite, relief worker and the last Vicereine of India; she was the wife of Louis Mountbatten, 1st Earl Mountbatten of Burma.
5th Apr	Peter Llewelyn Davies, MC (b. 25th February 1897) - The middle of five sons who were informally adopted by J. M. Barrie following the deaths of their parents, Arthur and Sylvia Llewelyn Davies. Barrie publicly identified Peter as the source of the name for the title character in his play Peter Pan. This public identification as 'the original Peter Pan' plagued Davies throughout his life.
1st May	Charles Henry Holden, Litt.D, FRIBA, MRTPI, RDI (b. 12th May 1875) - Architect best known for designing many London Underground stations during the 1920s and 1930s, Bristol Central Library, and the University of London's Senate House.

7th Jun	Sir Maurice Bonham-Carter, KCB, KCVO (b. 11th October 1880) - Liberal politician, civil servant and first-class cricketer widely known by the nickname Bongie.
27th Jun	Charlotte 'Lottie' Dod (b. 24th September 1871) - Sportswoman best known as a tennis player. She won the Wimbledon Ladies' Singles Championship five times, the first one when she was only fifteen years old in the summer of 1887. In addition to tennis she also won the British Ladies Amateur Golf Championship, played for the England women's national field hockey team (which she helped to found), and won a silver medal at the 1908 Summer Olympics in archery.
27th Jun	Harry Pollitt (b. 22nd November 1890) - Politician who served as the head of the trade union department of the Communist Party of Great Britain, and the General Secretary of the party.
6th Jul	Aneurin 'Nye' Bevan (b. 15th November 1897) - Welsh Labour Party politician and the Minister for Health from 1945 until 1951. Bevan is best remembered for spearheading the establishment of the National Health Service, to provide medical care free at point-of-need to all Britons regardless of wealth.
10th Aug	Frank William George Lloyd (b. 2nd February 1886) - Film director, actor, scriptwriter and producer who won Scotland's first ever Academy Award for his work on the silent film The Divine Lady (1929). Lloyd was among the founders of the Academy of Motion Picture Arts and Sciences, and was its president from 1934 to 1935.
22nd Sep	Melanie Klein (née Reizes, 30th March 1882) - Austrian-British author and psychoanalyst who is known for her work in child analysis. She was the primary figure in the development of object relations theory.
22nd Sep	Amy Veness (née Amy Clarice Beart; 26th February 1876) - Film actress known for her roles in Hobson's Choice (1931), Lorna Doone (1934) and Oliver Twist (1948).
27th Sep	Estelle Sylvia Pankhurst (b. 5th May 1882) - Campaigner for the suffragette movement and prominent left communist who was the daughter of Emmeline Pankhurst. She later became an activist in the cause of anti-fascism and spent much of her later life agitating on behalf of Ethiopia (where she eventually moved).
30th Sep	Harry St John Bridger Philby, CIE (b. 3rd April 1885) - Arabist, adviser, explorer, writer and colonial office intelligence officer, also known as Jack Philby or Sheikh Abdullah.
3rd Nov	Sir Harold Spencer Jones, KBE, FRS, FRSE, PRAS (b. 29th March 1890) - Astronomer who became renowned as an authority on positional astronomy and served as Astronomer Royal for 23 years.
16th Nov	Gilbert Harding (b. 5th June 1907) - Schoolmaster, journalist, policeman, disc-jockey, actor, interviewer and television presenter. He also appeared in several films, sometimes in character parts but usually as himself.
27th Nov	Frederick Luther Fane, MC (b. 27th April 1875) - Cricketer who played for Essex, Oxford University and London County. He also played for England in 14 Test matches and captained the team on five occasions. During the First World War Fane was commissioned in the West Yorkshire Regiment and was awarded the Military Cross 'for conspicuous gallantry and devotion to duty while commanding a patrol'.
22nd Dec	Sir John Ninian Comper (b. 10th June 1864) - Scottish-born architect who was one of the last of the great Gothic Revival architects, noted for his churches and their furnishings.

1960 TOP 10 SINGLES

Everly Brothers	No.1	Cathy's Clown
The Shadows	No.2	Apache
Cliff Richard	No.3	Please Don't Tease
Anthony Newley	No.4	Why
Shirley Bassey	No.5	As Long As He Needs Me
Roy Orbison	No.6	Only The Lonely
Elvis Presley	No.7	It's Now Or Never
Jimmy Jones	No.8	Handy Man
Elvis Presley	No.9	A Mess Of Blues
Jimmy Jones	No.10	Good Timin'

Everly Brothers
Cathy's Clown

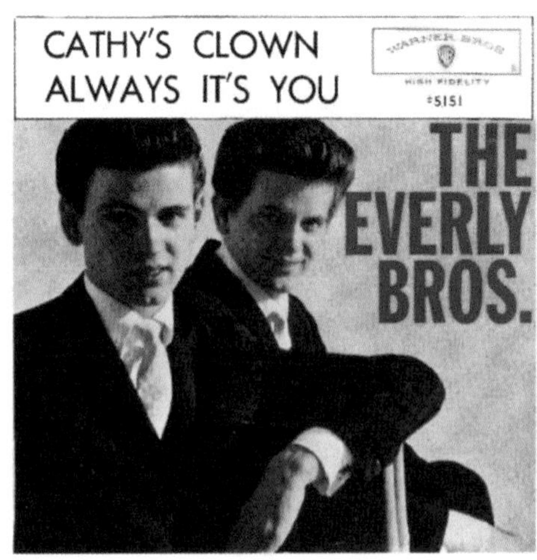

Label:	Written by:	Length:
Warner Bros. Records	D. Everly / P. Everly	2 mins 22 secs

The Everly Brothers, Isaac Donald 'Don' Everly (b. 1st February 1937) and Phillip 'Phil' Everly (b. 19th January 1939 - d. 3rd January 2014) were a country-influenced rock and roll duo known for steel-string acoustic guitar playing and close harmony singing. Between 1957 and 1984 they charted 30 singles in the U.K.; 29 in the Top 40, 13 in the Top 10, and 4 No.1's.

The Shadows
Apache

Label:	Written by:	Length:
Columbia	Jerry Lordan	2 mins 51 secs

The Shadows (originally known as the Drifters) were an instrumental rock group. They were Cliff Richard's backing band from 1958 to 1968, and during their career placed 69 singles in the U.K. charts. The Shadows are the fourth most successful act in the British chart history behind Elvis Presley, the Beatles and Cliff Richard.

Cliff Richard
Please Don't Tease

Label:	Written by:	Length:
Columbia	Welch / Chester	2 mins 59 secs

Sir Cliff Richard, OBE (b. Harry Rodger Webb; 14th October 1940) is a pop singer, musician, performer, actor and philanthropist who has total sales of over 21 million singles in the U.K., and over 250 million records worldwide. His single Please Don't Tease sold 1.59 million copies and reached the No.1 spot in India, Ireland, New Zealand, Norway and Thailand, in addition to the U.K.

Anthony Newley
Why?

Label:	Written by:	Length:
Decca	De Angelis / Marcucci	2 mins 29 secs

Anthony Newley (b. 24th September 1931 - d. 14th April 1999) was an actor, singer and songwriter. As a recording artist he enjoyed a dozen Top 40 entries on the U.K. Singles Chart between 1959 and 1962, including two No.1 hits. The Guinness Book of British Hit Singles & Albums describe Newley as "among the most innovative U.K. acts of the early rock years before moving into musicals and cabaret". He was inducted into the Songwriters Hall of Fame in 1989.

5 Shirley Bassey
As Long As He Needs Me

Label:	Written by:	Length:
Columbia	Lionel Bart	2 mins 59 secs

Dame Shirley Veronica Bassey, DBE (b. 8th January 1937) is a Welsh singer whose career began in the mid-1950s. She is best known both for her powerful voice and for recording the theme songs to the James Bond films Goldfinger (1964), Diamonds Are Forever (1971), and Moonraker (1979). In 1977 she received the Brit Award for Best British Female Solo Artist in the previous 25 years. As Long as He Needs Me was written by Lionel Bart (for the character of Nancy) in the 1960 musical Oliver!

6 Roy Orbison
Only The Lonely

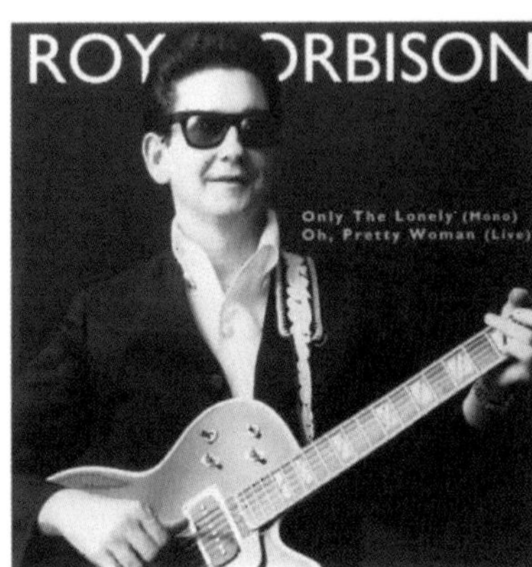

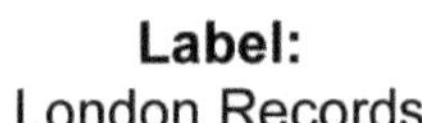

Label:	Written by:	Length:
London Records	Melson / Orbison	2 mins 22 secs

Roy Kelton Orbison (b. 23rd April 1936 - d. 6th December 1988) was an American singer, songwriter and musician known for his impassioned singing style, complex song structures, and dark emotional ballads. Only the Lonely was the first major hit for Orbison in the U.K and the first of 3 British No.1 records. His honours include being inducted into the Rock and Roll Hall of Fame in 1987, and the Songwriters Hall of Fame in 1989.

7 Elvis Presley
It's Now Or Never

Label:	**Written by:**	**Length:**
RCA Victor	Schroeder / Di Capua / Gold	3 mins 12 secs

Elvis Aaron Presley (b. 8th January 1935 - d. 16th August 1977) was an American singer and actor. Regarded as one of the most significant cultural icons and influential musicians of the 20th century, he is often referred to as 'the King of Rock and Roll', or simply, 'the King'. It's Now or Never, based on the Italian song O Sole Mio, is one of the best-selling singles of all time having sold in excess of 25 million copies worldwide. Its British release was delayed which allowed the song to build up massive advance orders and to enter the charts straight at No.1, a very rare occurrence at the time.

Jimmy Jones
Handy Man

Label:	**Written by:**	**Length:**
MGM Records	Jones / Blackwell	1 min 58 secs

James Jones (b. 2nd June 1937 - d. 2nd August 2012) was an American singer-songwriter who is best known for his smooth yet soulful falsetto modelled on the likes of Clyde McPhatter and Sam Cooke. Handy Man was co-written by Jones in 1955 and reworked by Otis Blackwell in 1959. It was Jones' first hit single and went to No.2 on the U.S. Billboard Hot 100 and peaked at No.3 in the U.K. Singles Chart.

Elvis Presley
A Mess Of Blues

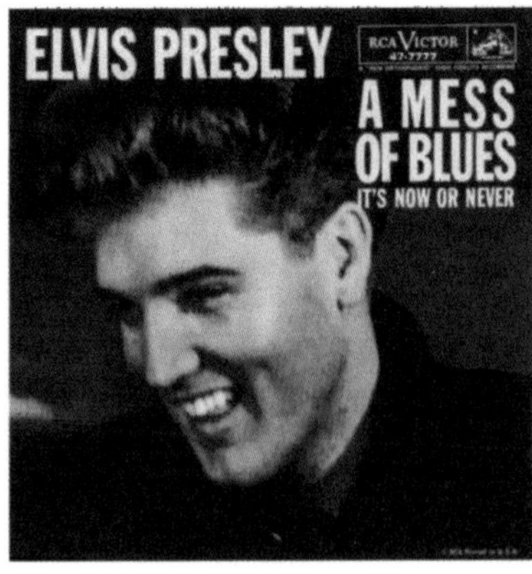

Label:	Written by:	Length:
RCA Victor	Pomus / Shuman	2 mins 40 secs

A Mess Of Blues, originally recorded by Elvis Presley for RCA Records as the B-side to It's Now or Never, became a hit independently in the U.K. and reached the No.2 spot in the charts. Commercially successful in many genres including rock and roll, pop, blues and gospel, Presley is the best-selling solo artist in the history of recorded music with estimated record sales in excess 600 million units worldwide. He won three Grammys and also received the Grammy Lifetime Achievement Award at the age of 36.

Jimmy Jones
Good Timin'

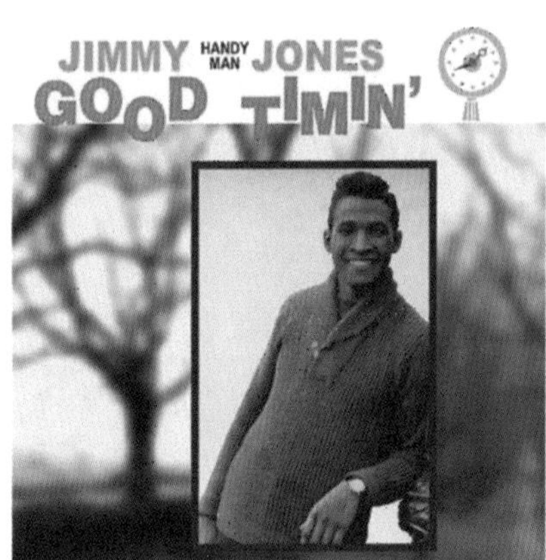

Label:	Written by:	Length:
MGM Records	Ballard Jr. / Tobias	2 mins 10 secs

Good Timin' climbed to No.1 in the U.K. charts in July 1960, just a few months after Jimmy Jones had secured his first hit record, Handy Man. Both these recordings were awarded gold disks after selling over one million copies each. Although these were Jones' only two Top 10 singles, he did have three more British chart entries in the following twelve months. Jones' subsequent career was low key although he did keep active in the music industry as both a songwriter and recording artist.

1960: TOP FILMS

1. **Swiss Family Robinson** - *Disney*
2. **Psycho** - *Paramount*
3. **Spartacus** - *Universal*
4. **Exodus** - *United Artists*
5. **The Apartment** - *United Artists*

OSCARS

Best Picture: The Apartment

Most Nominations: The Apartment (10)
Most Wins: The Apartment (5)

Photo 1: Elizabeth Taylor & Burt Lancaster / Photo 2: Peter Ustinov & Shirley Jones.

Best Director: Billy Wilder - *The Apartment*

Best Actor: Burt Lancaster - *Elmer Gantry*
Best Actress: Elizabeth Taylor - *Butterfield 8*
Best Supporting Actor: Peter Ustinov - *Spartacus*
Best Supporting Actress: Shirley Jones - *Elmer Gantry*

The 33rd Academy Awards were presented on Monday 17th April 1961 at the Santa Monica Civic Auditorium, Santa Monica, California.

SWISS FAMILY ROBINSON

Directed by: Ken Annakin - Runtime: 2 hours 6 minutes

A family are shipwrecked on route to New Guinea and must learn to survive on a deserted tropical island.

STARRING

John Mills
b. 22nd February 1908
d. 23rd April 2005

Character:
Father Robinson

English actor born Lewis Ernest Watts who appeared in more than 120 films in a career spanning seven decades. On screen he often played people who are not at all exceptional but become heroes because of their common sense, generosity and good judgment. He received an Academy Award for Best Supporting Actor for his work in Ryan's Daughter (1970).

Dorothy Hackett McGuire
b. 14th June 1916
d. 13th September 2001

Character:
Mother Robinson

American film, stage, television and radio actress. McGuire achieved Broadway fame when cast in the title role of the domestic comedy Claudia which ran for 722 performances from 1941 to 1943. In film she was nominated for the Academy Award for Best Actress for Gentleman's Agreement (1947) and won the National Board of Review Award for Best Actress for Friendly Persuasion (1956).

James Gordon MacArthur
b. 8th December 1937
d. 28th October 2010

Character:
Fritz Robinson

American actor best known for the role of Danny 'Danno' Williams in the long-running television series Hawaii Five-O, and for playing the juvenile lead in a series of Disney movies. In addition to film and television he also appeared on Broadway opposite Jane Fonda in Invitation To A March (1960), and released several records, scoring two minor Billboard Hot 100 hits.

Goofs

A reference to Napoleonic Wars places the film's setting between 1804 and 1815. Actress Janet Munro who plays Roberta is shown clearly wearing the straps of a 1950's-era brassiere.

When Fritz is wrestling the snake, Ernst charges in with a machete to assist him. The blade of the machete is seen flopping around revealing it to be a rubber prop.

When Fritz and Ernst are sailing, Ernst prepares to write in a journal by licking his quill pen as if it were a pencil. He does not dip it in ink.

CONTINUED

Interesting Facts

Director Ken Annakin revealed that the trapped zebra in the film was subjected to electric shocks to make it move about, a practice that would be illegal in Hollywood movies today.

Although set in a tropical paradise the filming in Tobago was considerably hampered by almost constant rain.

Walt Disney Pictures bought the rights to the 1940 version of Swiss Family Robinson distributed by RKO. Walt Disney then confiscated all known prints of RKO Radio Pictures' version so there wouldn't be any comparisons to the Disney version.

Neither Roberta nor the pirates appear in Johann David Wyss's 1812 novel on which this film was based.

Duke, one of the Robinson's guardian Great Danes, appeared in The Ugly Dachshund (1966).

A huge fan of this movie, Star Wars creator George Lucas named Anakin Skywalker after director Ken Annakin.

Quotes

Father: Don't you sometimes feel that this is the kind of life we were meant to live on this earth? Everything we need, everything, right here, right at our fingertips. You know, if only people could have all this and be satisfied, I don't think there'd be any real problems in the world.

Father: The world is full of nice, ordinary little people who live in nice, ordinary little houses on the ground. But didn't you ever dream of a house up on a tree top?
Mother: No! Mostly I dream of having a house in New Guinea.

PSYCHO

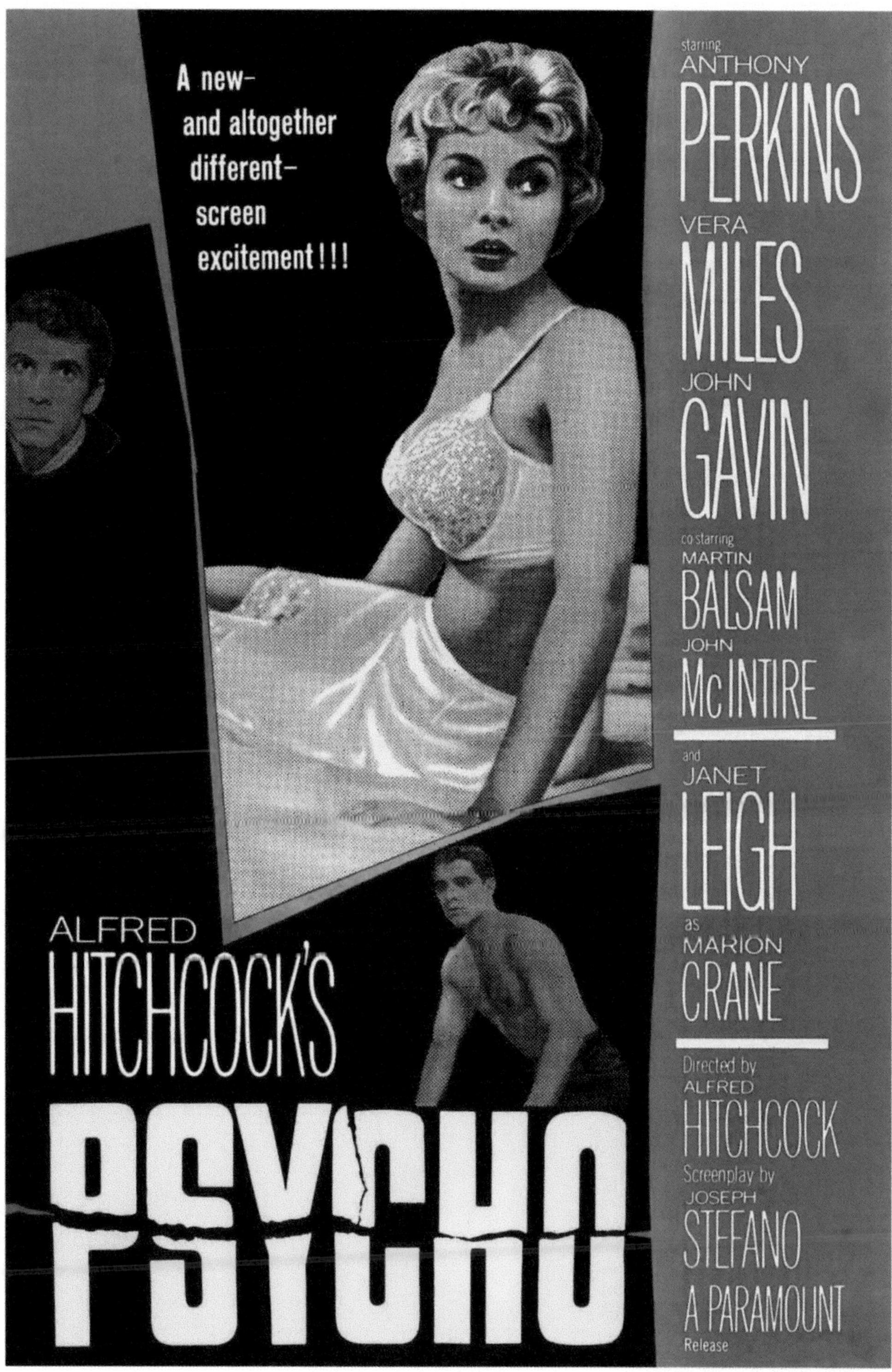

Directed by: Alfred Hitchcock - Runtime: 1 hour 49 minutes

A Phoenix secretary embezzles forty thousand dollars from her employer's client, goes on the run, and checks into a remote motel run by a young man who seems to be dominated by his mother.

STARRING

Anthony Perkins
b. 4th April 1932
d. 12th September 1992

Character:
Norman Bates

American actor and singer who first came to the public's attention for his second film, Friendly Persuasion (1956), for which he was nominated for the Academy Award for Best Supporting Actor and for which he received the Golden Globe Award for New Star of the Year - Actor. Perkins is best remembered though for playing Norman Bates in Alfred Hitchcock's Psycho and its three sequels.

Vera Miles
b. 23rd August 1929

Character:
Lila Crane

Retired American actress who worked closely with Alfred Hitchcock, most notably as Lila Crane in Psycho, a role she reprised in Psycho II (1983). Other films in which she has appeared include Tarzan's Hidden Jungle (1955), The Searchers (1956), The Wrong Man (1956), The Man Who Shot Liberty Valance (1962), Follow Me, Boys! (1966), Sergeant Ryker (1968), and Molly and Lawless John (1972).

John Gavin
b. 8th April 1931
d. 9th February 2018

Character:
Sam Loomis

American actor born Juan Vincent Apablasa Jr. who was also notably the president of the Screen Actors Guild (1971-1973), and the U.S. Ambassador to Mexico (1981-1986). Gavin's break came as the lead in A Time to Love and a Time to Die (1958). He is best known for his performances in the films Imitation of Life (1959), Spartacus (1960), Psycho (1960), and Thoroughly Modern Millie (1967).

Goofs

At the car dealership the same extras can be seen repeatedly walking in different directions.

When Norman meets Marion his first words to her are an apology for not hearing her on account of the rain, before then asking her to accompany him into the office. He does all this without moving his lips.

Interesting Facts

Director Alfred Hitchcock bought the screen rights to the novel Psycho anonymously from Robert Bloch for only $9,500.

CONTINUED

Interesting Facts	Alfred Hitchcock was so pleased with the score written by Bernard Herrmann, that he doubled the composer's salary to $34,501. Hitchcock later said, "Thirty-three percent of the effect of Psycho was due to the music". A shot of Marion removing her black bra before her shower was removed by the U.S. censors, while the scene remained intact in the U.K. Alfred Hitchcock wanted to make this movie so much that he deferred his standard $250,000 salary in lieu of 60% of the movie's gross. Paramount Pictures, believing that this movie would do poorly at the box-office, agreed. His personal earnings from this movie exceeded $15 million. Adjusted for inflation that would amount to just over $130 million today. Walt Disney refused to allow Alfred Hitchcock to film at Disneyland in the early 1960s because Hitchcock had made "that disgusting movie, Psycho".
Quote	**Marion Crane:** Do you go out with friends? **Norman Bates:** A boy's best friend is his mother.

SPARTACUS

Directed by: Stanley Kubrick - Runtime: 3 hours 17 minutes

A proud and gifted Thracian slave named Spartacus leads a violent revolt against a decadent Roman Republic.

STARRING

Kirk Douglas
b. 9th December 1916

Character:
Spartacus

Born Issur Danielovitch, Douglas is a retired actor, producer, director and author. His film debut came in The Strange Love of Martha Ivers (1946) with Barbara Stanwyck. In the 1950s and 1960s Douglas developed into a leading box-office star and during his sixty-year acting career he has appeared in over 90 films. Douglas has received three Academy Award nominations and in 1996 received Lifetime Achievement Oscar.

Laurence Olivier
b. 22nd May 1907
d. 11th July 1989

Character:
Crassus

Actor and director who dominated the British stage of the mid-20th century. He also worked in films throughout his career playing more than fifty cinema roles. For his on-screen work he received four Academy Awards, two British Academy Film Awards, five Emmy Awards and three Golden Globe Awards. He is also commemorated in the Laurence Olivier Awards given annually by the Society of London Theatre.

Jean Merilyn Simmons
b. 31st January 1929
d. 22nd January 2010

Character:
Varinia

British-American actress and singer who appeared predominantly in films, beginning with those made in Great Britain during and after World War II, followed mainly by Hollywood films from 1950 onwards. Simmons was nominated for the Academy Award for Best Supporting Actress for Hamlet (1948), and won a Golden Globe Award for Best Actress for Guys and Dolls (1955).

Goofs

During the scene where the slaves are storming a wall, the slaves who die at the wall can be seen rolling under it to jump over again later.

Many of the horsemen use stirrups, an invention which did not reach Europe until the 7th century A.D., eight centuries after the film is set.

Interesting Facts

Stanley Kubrick was brought in as director after Kirk Douglas had a major falling out with the original director, Anthony Mann. According to Sir Peter Ustinov (who played Batiatus) the salt mines sequence is the only footage shot by Mann.

CONTINUED

Interesting Facts	The original version included a scene where Marcus Licinius Crassus (Sir Laurence Olivier) attempts to seduce Antoninus (Tony Curtis). The Production Code Administration and the Legion of Decency both objected. In the end the scene was cut, but it was put back in for the 1991 restoration. In order to get so many big stars to play supporting roles, Kirk Douglas showed each a different script in which their character was emphasised. Winning a Best Actor in a Supporting Role Oscar for his portrayal of Batiatus, Sir Peter Ustinov stands as the only actor to win an Oscar for a Stanley Kubrick movie. Jean Simmons recalled a long day of filming where it took forever to get Kirk Douglas on the cross for his crucifixion. When he was up, the assistant director called lunch and left him there.
Quotes	**Antoninus:** I'm Spartacus! *[everyone around Antoninus and Spartacus takes up the shout]* *[being forced to fight]* **Spartacus:** Don't give them the pleasure of a contest. Lower your guard, I'll kill you on the first rush. **Antoninus:** I won't let them crucify you! Spartacus: It's my last order, obey it!

EXODUS

Directed by: Otto Preminger - Runtime: 3 hours 28 minutes

Fictional but fact-based account of the struggle for the emergence of modern Israel as an independent country.

STARRING

Paul Newman
b. 26th January 1925
d. 26th September 2008

Character:
Ari Ben Canaan

American actor, IndyCar driver, entrepreneur, activist, and philanthropist. He won numerous acting awards including an Oscar for his role in the 1986 film The Color Of Money. He starred in many other classic films including The Hustler (1961), Cool Hand Luke (1967), Butch Cassidy and the Sundance Kid (1969), and The Sting (1973). Newman co-founded food company Newman's Own which has so far donated over US$485 million to charity.

Eva Marie Saint
b. 4th July 1924

Character:
Kitty Fremont

American actress with a career spanning 70 years. She is known for starring in Elia Kazan's On the Waterfront (1954), for which she won an Academy Award for Best Supporting Actress, and Alfred Hitchcock's North by Northwest (1959). She received Golden Globe and BAFTA Award nominations for A Hatful of Rain (1957), and was the winner of a Primetime Emmy Award for the television miniseries People Like Us (1990).

Ralph Richardson
b. 19th December 1902
d. 10th October 1983

Character:
General Sutherland

English actor who, along with his contemporaries Peggy Ashcroft, John Gielgud, and Laurence Olivier, dominated the British stage of the mid-20th century. He worked in films throughout most of his career and played more than sixty cinema roles. He was twice nominated for an Oscar for Best Supporting Actor, first for The Heiress (1949) and again for his final film, Greystoke: The Legend of Tarzan, Lord of the Apes (1984).

Goofs

Early in Exodus, Kitty appears wearing a square dress outfit with no sleeves and bare underarms, a fashion totally out of place in 1947.

When Ari gets out of the car his head hits the corner of the door and he touches his forehead. Eva Marie Saint barely restrains her laughter.

Interesting Facts

This film has been credited with stimulating support for Zionism and the state of Israel in the United States.

CONTINUED

Interesting Facts

Paul Newman and producer and director Otto Preminger did not get along while making this movie. Preminger was not interested in hearing Newman's ideas. Newman later said he regretted making the movie.

The production company hired two hundred fifty extras to play escaping prisoners at the old prison in Acre. However, two hundred fifty-three people were counted as escaping, the extra three were actual escapees from a mental ward near the set.

Paul Newman took the part of Ari Ben Canaan in honour of his father who was Jewish.

At the premiere, as the film neared its third hour with the end not yet in sight, comedian Mort Sahl stood up from his seat in the packed theatre and shouted, "Otto Preminger, let my people go!" The incident quickly became a popular piece of Hollywood lore.

Quote

Ari Ben Canaan: *[Talking to Kitty, aboard the ship]* Each person onboard this ship is a soldier. The only weapon we have to fight with is our willingness to die.

THE APARTMENT

Directed by: Billy Wilder - Runtime: 2 hours 5 minutes

A man tries to rise in his company by letting its executives use his apartment for trysts, but complications and a romance of his own ensue.

Starring

Jack Lemmon
b. 8th February 1925
d. 27th June 2001

Character:
C.C. Baxter

American actor and musician who starred in over 60 films including Mister Roberts (1955), Some Like It Hot (1959), The Great Race (1965), The Odd Couple (1968) and its sequel 30 years later, Save the Tiger (1973), The China Syndrome (1979), Missing (1982) and Grumpy Old Men (1993). Lemmon was nominated eight times for an Oscar, winning twice for his roles in Mister Roberts and Save The Tiger.

Shirley MacLaine
b. 24th April 1934

Characters:
Fran Kubelik

American film, television, and theatre actress, singer, dancer, activist, and author who won an Academy Award for Terms of Endearment (1983). MacLaine also received the 40th Life Achievement Award from the American Film Institute in 2012, and received the Kennedy Center Honors for her lifetime contributions to American culture through the performing arts in 2013.

Fred MacMurray
b. 30th August 1908
d. 5th November 1991

Character:
Jeff D. Sheldrake

American actor who appeared in more than 100 films during a career that spanned nearly half a century (1929-1978). MacMurray is best known for his roles in the film Double Indemnity (1944), for his performances in numerous Disney films including The Shaggy Dog (1959) and The Absent-Minded Professor (1961), and as Steve Douglas in the television series My Three Sons which ran from 1960 to 1972.

Goofs

During the opening panorama of the New York skyline, with the United Nations Building in the foreground, the shot shown is mirror-image of the actual scene.

Whilst playing Gin Rummy Fran's hair keeps shifting and changing throughout the scene.

Interesting Facts

This was the last black and white film to win Best Picture at The Academy Awards until The Artist (2011); Schindler's List (1993), which won in 1994, although shot black and white did have some scenes in colour.

CONTINUED

Interesting Facts Shirley MacLaine was initially only given forty pages of the film script because director Billy Wilder didn't want her to know how the story would turn out. She thought it was because the script wasn't finished.

Jack Lemmon said he learned much about filmmaking from Billy Wilder, particularly the director's use of 'hooks', bits of business the audience remembers long after they've forgotten other aspects of the movie. One such hook was the passing of the key to Baxter's apartment. Lemmon said for years after the picture's release people would come up to him and say, "Hey, Jack, can I have the key?"

For The Apartment, Billy Wilder became the first person to win the Academy Awards for Best Picture, Best Director and Best Screenplay.

Quotes **C.C. Baxter:** Ya know, I used to live like Robinson Crusoe; I mean, shipwrecked among 8 million people. And then one day I saw a footprint in the sand, and there you were.

Fran Kubelik: Why do people have to love people anyway?

[last lines]
C.C. Baxter: You hear what I said, Miss Kubelik? I absolutely adore you.
Fran Kubelik: Shut up and deal...

SPORTING WINNERS

BBC SPORTS PERSONALITY OF THE YEAR

DAVID BROOME - SHOW JUMPING

David McPherson Broome, CBE (b. 1st March 1940) is a retired Welsh show jumping champion who competed in the 1960, 1964, 1968, 1972 and 1988 Olympics, and won individual bronze medals in 1960 and 1968 on his best-known horse Mr Softee.

Major Championship Medals:

Year	Competition	Location	Event	Medal
1960	Olympic Games	Rome	Individual Jumping	Bronze
1960	World Championships	Venice	Individual Jumping	Bronze
1961	European Championships	Aachen	Individual Jumping	Gold
1967	European Championships	Rotterdam	Individual Jumping	Gold
1968	Olympic Games	Mexico	Individual Jumping	Bronze
1969	European Championships	Hickstead	Individual Jumping	Gold
1970	World Championships	La Baule	Individual Jumping	Gold
1977	European Championships	Vienna	Team Jumping	Silver
1978	World Championships	Aachen	Team Jumping	Gold
1979	European Championships	Rotterdam	Team Jumping	Gold
1982	World Championships	Dublin	Team Jumping	Bronze
1983	European Championships	Hickstead	Team Jumping	Silver
1990	World Championships	Stockholm	Team Jumping	Bronze
1991	European Championships	La Baule	Team Jumping	Silver

Broome turned professional in 1973, and in 1978 helped the British team to win the World Championship. In addition to his numerous major championship medals he has also won the King George V Gold Cup a record six times (on six different horses) between 1960-1991, a record yet to be equalled.

Five Nations Rugby Winners

France & England

Position	Nation	Played	Won	Draw	Lost	For	Against	+/-	Points
1	**France**	**4**	**3**	**1**	**0**	**55**	**28**	**+27**	**7**
1	**England**	**4**	**3**	**1**	**0**	**46**	**26**	**+20**	**7**
3	Wales	4	2	0	2	32	39	-7	4
4	Scotland	4	1	0	3	29	47	-18	2
5	Ireland	4	0	0	4	25	47	-22	0

The 1960 Five Nations Championship was the thirty-first series of the rugby union Five Nations Championship. Including the previous incarnations as the Home Nations and Five Nations, this was the sixty-sixth series of the northern hemisphere rugby union championship.

Date	Team		Score		Team	Location
09-01-1960	Scotland		11-13		France	Edinburgh
16-01-1960	England		14-6		Wales	London
06-02-1960	Wales		8-0		Scotland	Cardiff
13-02-1960	England		8-5		Ireland	London
27-02-1960	France		3-3		England	Paris
27-02-1960	Ireland		5-6		Scotland	Dublin
12-03-1960	Ireland		9-10		Wales	Dublin
19-03-1960	Scotland		12-21		England	Edinburgh
26-03-1960	Wales		8-16		France	Cardiff
09-04-1960	France		23-6		Ireland	Paris

Calcutta Cup

Scotland 12 - 21 England

The Calcutta Cup was first awarded in 1879 and is the rugby union trophy awarded to the winner of the match (currently played as part of the Six Nations Championship) between England and Scotland. The Cup was presented to the Rugby Football Union after the Calcutta Football Club in India disbanded in 1878; it is made from melted down silver rupees withdrawn from the club's funds.

British Grand Prix - Jack Brabham

Jack Brabham takes the chequered flag in his Cooper-Climax to win the British Grand Prix.

The 1960 British Grand Prix was held at Silverstone on the 16th July. The race was won by reigning World Champion Jack Brabham, from pole position, over 77 laps of the 2.927-mile circuit. The fastest lap was taken by Graham Hill with a time of 1m 34.4s on lap 56.

Pos.	Country	Driver	Car
1	**Australia**	**Jack Brabham**	**Cooper-Climax**
2	United Kingdom	John Surtees	Lotus-Climax
3	United Kingdom	Innes Ireland	Lotus-Climax

1960 Grand Prix Season

Date	Race	Circuit	Winning Driver	Constructor
07-02	Argentine Grand Prix	Buenos Aires	Bruce McLaren	Cooper-Climax
29-05	Monaco Grand Prix	Monaco	Stirling Moss	Lotus-Climax
30-05	Indianapolis 500	Indianapolis	Jim Rathmann	Watson-Offenhauser
06-06	Dutch Grand Prix	Zandvoort	Jack Brabham	Cooper-Climax
19-06	Belgian Grand Prix	Spa	Jack Brabham	Cooper-Climax
03-07	French Grand Prix	Reims	Jack Brabham	Cooper-Climax
16-07	British Grand Prix	Silverstone	Jack Brabham	Cooper-Climax
14-08	Portuguese Grand Prix	Boavista	Jack Brabham	Cooper-Climax
04-09	Italian Grand Prix	Monza	Phil Hill	Ferrari
20-11	U.S. Grand Prix	Riverside	Stirling Moss	Lotus-Climax

The 1960 Formula One season was the fourteenth season of the FIA's Formula One motor racing. It featured the eleventh FIA World Championship of Drivers, the third International Cup for F1 Manufacturers and numerous non-championship Formula One races. Jack Brabham won his second consecutive title with 43 points from Bruce McLaren (34) and Stirling Moss (19).

Grand National - Merryman II

The 1960 Grand National was the 114th renewal of this world famous horse race and took place at Aintree Racecourse near Liverpool on the 26th March. The winning horse was Merryman II who was trained by Neville Crump and ridden by 22-year old jockey Gerry Scott.

Of the 26 horses that contested the race only 8 completed it; 11 fell, 3 pulled up, 2 refused and 2 unseated their riders.

Photo: Gerry Scott riding Merryman II past the winning post in the 1960 Grand National.

	Horse	Jockey	Age	Weight	Odds
1st	**Merryman II**	**Gerry Scott**	**9**	**10st-12lb**	**13/2**
2nd	Badanloch	Stan Mellor	9	10st-9lb	100/7
3rd	Clear Profit	Jumbo Wilkinson	10	10st-1lb	20/1
4th	Tea Fiend	Gerry Madden	11	10st-0lb	33/1
5th	Sabaria	Mick Roberts	9	10st-3lb	66/1

Epsom Derby - St. Paddy

The Derby Stakes is Britain's richest horse race and the most prestigious of the country's five Classics. First run in 1780 this Group 1 flat horse race is open to 3-year-old thoroughbred colts and fillies. The race takes place at Epsom Downs in Surrey over a distance of one mile, four furlongs and 10 yards (2,423 metres) and is scheduled for early June each year.

Photo: British Thoroughbred racehorse and sire St. Paddy (1957-1984) seen being led in after winning the 1960 Epsom Derby. The horse was owned by Sir Victor Sassoon, trained by Noel Murless and ridden by Lester Piggott.

FOOTBALL LEAGUE CHAMPIONS

England

Pos.	Team	W	D	L	F	A	Pts.
1	**Burnley**	**24**	**7**	**11**	**85**	**61**	**55**
2	Wolverhampton Wanderers	24	6	12	106	67	54
3	Tottenham Hotspur	21	11	10	86	50	53
4	West Bromwich Albion	19	11	12	83	57	49
5	Sheffield Wednesday	19	11	12	80	59	49

Scotland

Pos.	Team	W	D	L	F	A	Pts.
1	**Heart of Midlothian**	**23**	**8**	**3**	**102**	**51**	**54**
2	Kilmarnock	24	2	8	67	45	50
3	Rangers	17	8	9	72	38	42
4	Dundee	16	10	8	70	49	42
5	Motherwell	16	8	10	71	61	40

FA CUP WINNERS

Blackburn Rovers 0-3 Wolverhampton Wanderers

The 1960 FA Cup Final took place on the 7th May at Wembley Stadium in front of 98,954 fans. Wolves took the cup for the fourth time after an own goal from Blackburn defender Mick McGrath and two goals from winger Norman Deeley. *Fun fact: This was the first time the FA Cup winners would earn a place in a European competition, the newly formed Cup Winners' Cup.*

County Championship Cricket Winners

Yorkshire

The 1960 County Championship was the 61st officially organised running of the cricket competition and saw Yorkshire win their second successive title.

Pos.	Team	Played	Points	Average
1	**Yorkshire**	**32**	**246**	**7.68**
2	Lancashire	32	214	6.68
3	Middlesex	28	186	6.64
4	Sussex	32	188	5.87
5	Derbyshire	28	152	5.42

Test Series Cricket

England 3-0 South Africa

Test	Ground	Result
1st Test	Edgbaston, Birmingham	England won by 100 runs
2nd Test	Lord's, London	England won by an innings and 73 runs
3rd Test	Trent Bridge, Nottingham	England won by 8 wickets
4th Test	Old Trafford, Manchester	Match drawn
5th Test	The Oval, London	Match drawn

Golf - Open Championship - Kel Nagle

The 1960 Open Championship was the 89th to be played and was held between the 6th and 9th July at the Old Course in St Andrews, Scotland. Australian Kel Nagle prevailed over American Arnold Palmer by a single stroke to take his only major championship victory and £1,250 in prize money.

Photo: Kel Nagle celebrates with the Claret Jug after winning the 1960 Open.

WIMBLEDON

Photo 1: Neale Fraser being presented with his men's singles trophy. Photo 2: Maria Bueno holds the victor's trophy plate after winning the women's singles final.

Men's Singles Champion Neale Fraser - Australia
Ladies Singles Champion - Maria Bueno - Brazil

The 1960 Wimbledon Championships was the 74th staging of tournament and took place on the outdoor grass courts at the All England Lawn Tennis and Croquet Club in Wimbledon, London. It ran from the 20th June until the 2nd July and was the third Grand Slam tennis event of 1960.

Men's Singles Final:

Country	Player	Set 1	Set 2	Set 3	Set 4
Australia	Neale Fraser	6	3	9	7
Australia	Rod Laver	4	6	7	5

Women's Singles Final:

Country	Player	Set 1	Set 2
Brazil	Maria Bueno	8	6
South Africa	Sandra Reynolds	6	0

Men's Doubles Final:

Country	Players	Set 1	Set 2	Set 3
Mexico / United States	Rafael Osuna / Dennis Ralston	7	6	10
United Kingdom	Mike Davies / Bobby Wilson	5	3	8

Women's Doubles Final:

Country	Players	Set 1	Set 2
Brazil / United States	Maria Bueno / Darlene Hard	6	6
South Africa	Sandra Reynolds / Renée Schuurman	4	0

Mixed Doubles Final:

Country	Players	Set 1	Set 2	Set 3
Australia / United States	Rod Laver / Darlene Hard	13	3	8
Australia / Brazil	Robert Howe / Maria Bueno	11	6	6

1960 Summer Olympics

The 1960 Summer Olympics, officially known as the Games of the XVII Olympiad, were held in Rome, Italy between the 25th August and 11th September. A total of 5,338 athletes from 83 countries participated in these Games, competing in 150 events in 17 sports. *Fun fact: The city of Rome had previously been awarded the administration of the 1908 Summer Olympics, but following the eruption of Mount Vesuvius in 1906, Rome had no choice but to decline and pass the honour to London.*

British Gold Medallists:

Competitor	Discipline	Event
Don Thompson	Athletics	Men's 50km Walk
Anita Lonsbrough	Swimming	Women's 200m Breaststroke

Great Britain, represented by the British Olympic Association (BOA), took 253 competitors to Rome. The 206 men and 47 women took part in 130 events in 17 sports. The Rome Games continued Great Britain and Northern Ireland's disappointing run in the Olympics, with British athletes picking up only two gold medals (down from six in 1956).

Olympic Medals Table - Top 5 Countries:

Rank	Nation	Gold	Silver	Bronze	Total
1	Soviet Union	43	29	31	103
2	United States	34	21	16	71
3	Italy	13	10	13	36
4	United Team of Germany	12	19	11	42
5	Australia	8	8	6	22
12	**Great Britain**	**2**	**6**	**12**	**20**

The Cost Of Living

Comparison Chart

	1960	1960 (+ Inflation)	2019	% Change
3 Bedroom House	£3,550	£81,239	£236,676	+191.3
Weekly Income	£7.18s.8d	£181.55	£569	+213.4
Pint Of Beer	1s.1d	£1.24	£3.69	+197.6
Cheese (lb)	3s.4d	£3.81	£3.09	-18.9
Bacon (lb)	4s	£4.58	£2.65	-42.1
Comic - Beano	2d	19p	£2.75	+1347.4

Start the day the Andrews way with that enviable spring-clean feeling

WHY SHOULD *you* miss the nicest way to start the morning? Drink Andrews. Treat yourself to a big, cool, clear, clean, bubbling glassful of Andrews. Let those champagne-bubbles sweep away every trace of morning muzziness. Make *your* mouth feel fresh as springtime. Give *you* that sparkling, *enviable*, spring-clean feeling.

And don't forget Andrews Inner Cleanliness. Because while sparkling Andrews is freshening your mouth it's also toning up your liver. Settling any little stomach upset. And it has the kindest way of keeping your system regular.

So – start the day the nicest way – the Andrews way – with that sparkling *spring-clean* feeling. That's the way to greet the morning. From now on.

Save on the big tin—it costs only 2/11. And don't forget to keep it handy—where all the family can help themselves.

Andrews for inner cleanliness

SHOPPING

Whipped Bon-Bons (¼lb)	5d
Liquorice Allsorts (¼lb)	4d
Hacks Medicated Sweets (¼lb)	1s
Victory V Lozenges (pkt.)	6d
Romance Milk Chocolate Bar	9d
Cadbury's Roses Chocolates (½lb box)	5s.6d
Royal Lemon Pie Filling	9d
Nescafe Instant Coffee (8oz tin)	11s.9d
Camp Coffee (small)	1s.3½d
Co-op 99 Tea (4oz)	1s.9d
Robinsons Trio Squash	2s.9d
Spree Orange / Lemon Squash (sachet)	4d
Peek Frean's Shortcake Biscuit (pkt.)	11½d
Beecham's Powders (single)	3d
Crookes Halibut Oil Capsules (30)	2s.6d
Cleer Nose Spray	3s.9d
PAL Injecto-Matic Safety Razor + 12 Blades	3s.6d
Old Spice Aftershave	6s.2d
Vosene Medicated Shampoo (large size)	2s.3d
Loxene Medicated Hair Cream	2s
Jey Pine Disinfectant Antiseptic (small bottle)	11d
Spratt's Mixed Ovals Dog Biscuits (large pkt.)	1s.11d

Here's great news for you!

'CAMP' PRICES ARE DOWN

Now 1/3½d · 2/5d · 5/9d

If you like coffee you'll love 'CAMP'

The finest of fine leaf teas

NINETY NINE

One of the many choice blends of

CO-OP TEA

enjoyed by MILLIONS daily

FROM CO-OPERATIVE STORES

CLOTHES

Women's Clothing

Sugden's Beaver Lamb Fur Coat	£19.17s.6d
Plastic Raincoat	5s.11d
Brookewear Permanently Pleated Dress	£3.7s.6d
Fairway House Rayon Afghalaine Dress	£2.3s.6d
Brookewear Tricel Full Circular Skirt	£2.10s
Fairway House Dressing Gown	£1.8s.6d
Spun Rayon Pyjamas	£1.7s.11d
Sarongster Girdle	£2.2s
Ambrose Wilson Corset	18s.9d
Woolworth's Crepe Slip	6s.11d
Nylon Lace Platform Padded Bra	19s.6d
Unlined Fabric Gloves	1s.11d
Ladies Casual Canvas Shoes	5s.11d

Men's Clothing

Royal Airforce Stormcoat (short length)	£2.19s.6d
Austin Reed Casual Tweed Jacket	£12.10s
Fairway House Dressing Gown	£1.8s.6d
Double Two Terylene Shirt	£3.3s
Woolworth's White Shirt	7s
Austin Reed Tapered Worsted Trousers	£6
Woolworth's Socks	1s.11d
Handkerchiefs	9d

CHILDREN - TOYS

Hercules Ranger Sports Bicycle	£13.10s
Pure Nylon Waterproof Wigwam	£1.3s.6d
Pride & Clark Electric Train Set	£2.19s.6d
Suedette Cowboy Suit	£1.5s
Child's De-Luxe Typewriter	£1.11s.11d
Maystan Child's Record Player	£1.18s.3d
Subbuteo Table Soccer	from 9s.11d
American Christmas Stocking	3s.11d
Everest Geometry Set	19s.9d

ELECTRICAL ITEMS

21in Philips Videomatic TV With Remote Control	72gns
McMichael Slim 17in Portable TV	57gns
AEG Table Top Refrigerator Model 120 (4½cu.ft.)	63gns
GEC Supreme 4-Plate Electric Cooker	£79
AEG Spin Dryer	23gns
Imperial Vacuum Cleaner	£6.6s
Vactric P590 Vacuum Cleaner	7gns
Norvic Corona Double Electric Blanket	£7.17s
GEC Superspeed Kettle	£3.15s
GEC Coffee Percolator	£8.1s.6d
Hoover Steam Iron	£4.12s.1d
Marianne Portable Transistor Radio	10gns
Remington Electric Shaver	£10.13s

FIRST ▼ FOLD

FLAP 'A'

THIRD ▼ FOLD

SECOND ▼ FOLD

The 'IDEAL' Christmas present

BELL

PORTABLE ALL-ELECTRIC SEWING MACHINE

Housewives the world over acclaim the Bell all-electric portable sewing machine, now offered at the amazingly low price of 12 guineas.
The Bell is a neat, compact and super efficient machine of revolutionary design with a built-in needle light and totally enclosed motor for complete protection. Write today for fully descriptive leaflet.

12 gns CASH

or £2.10.6 deposit and 96 weekly payments of 2/6.

★ TOTALLY ENCLOSED MOTOR
★ CENTRAL ROUND BOBBIN
★ VARIABLE TENSION CONTROL
★ FOOT CONTROL FOR SPEED REGULATION
★ BUILT-IN NEEDLE LIGHT
★ LUXURY CARRYING CASE
★ FULLY GUARANTEED AND SERVICED THROUGHOUT GREAT BRITAIN

FOR EVERY PURCHASER -A £1 CHRISTMAS BONUS

One pound will be allowed off every Bell Sewing Machine purchased as a result of this advertisement.

FOLD HERE

INSTRUCTIONS

1 Make sure your name and address is shown clearly.
2 Cut out the whole of this folder along dotted lines.
3 Fold as indicated and tuck FLAP A into FLAP B.
4 Make sure folding brings I.S.M. address outside and post today. (No stamp required)

POST TODAY

Telephone: ELGar 1315/6 or post this coupon

Post me details of the Bell Portable Sewing Machine without obligation to purchase.

NAME ....

ADDRESS ....

TYX1.

FIRST FOLD ALONG THIS LINE

CUT ▲ HERE

NO POSTAGE STAMP NECESSARY IF POSTED IN GREAT BRITAIN OR NORTHERN IRELAND

POSTAGE WILL BE PAID BY IDEAL SEWING MACHINE CO. LTD.

BUSINESS REPLY SERVICE
Licence No. MR2148

IDEAL SEWING MACHINE CO. LTD.
803, GREAT WESTERN TRADING ESTATE,
PARK ROYAL,
LONDON, N.W.10

FLAP 'B'

OTHER PRICES

Skoda Felicia Car	£744
Vauxhall Victor Car	£716.10s.10d
2 Week Holiday - Costa Brava, Spain (including flights)	£42.13s
8 Day Holiday - Nice, France (by rail)	£25.8s
9 Day Holiday - Germany (by coach)	19½gns
7 Day Holiday - Prestatyn, Wales (all inclusive)	£8.5s
London To Jersey (return flight)	£5.12s
Qualcast Super Panther Lawn Mower	£8.12s.6d
Norman Super Sabre 5-Speed Bicycle	£19.19s
Kitchen Table & 4 Chairs	13½gns
Shackleton's Double Sized Divan Bed	£13.10s
Brown Bros & Taylor Fireside Chairs (pair)	11½gns
Kosset Patterned Carpet (sq.yd.)	£2
Fleetway Carpet Sweeper	£2.3s.6d
LEO De-Luxe Oil Heater	£13.18s
J.A. Davis & Son Air Rifle	£5.8s.6d
Readicut Make Your Own Rug Outfit	from £1.15s
Whitehall Shockproof Pocket Watch	18s.6d
Platignum Writing Set	9s.6d
Black & White Scotch Whisky (large bottle)	£1.17s.6d
Captain Morgan Rum (large bottle)	£1.18s
Seager's Australian Port Style Wine	9s.6d
Nelson Tipped Cigarettes (50)	8s.9d
Picador Pocket Size Cigars (10)	4s.1d
Woman's Weekly Magazine	5d

Money Conversion Table

1960 'Old Money'		Value	2019
Farthing	¼d	0.1p	2½p
Half Penny	½d	0.21p	5p
Penny	1d	0.42p	10p
Threepence	3d	1.25p	29p
Sixpence	6d	2.5p	57p
Shilling	1s	5p	£1.14
Florin	2s	10p	£2.29
Half Crown	2s.6d	12.5p	£2.86
Crown	5s	25p	£5.72
Ten Shillings	10s	50p	£11.44
Pound	20s	£1	£22.88
Guinea	21s	£1.05	£24.03
Five Pounds	£5	£5	£114.42
Ten Pounds	£10	£10	£228.84

They'll really enjoy

HARRIS Wiltshire Sausages

...FOR BREAKFAST There's no better way for your family to start the day. The delicious fragrance and flavour of sizzling Harris Wiltshire Sausages gives them that 'rarin'-to-go' feeling ... means they face the day happy and satisfied with a meal that's really nourishing. Harris Wiltshire Sausages, made to a unique recipe, contain more meat ... giving a best-you-ever-tasted flavour that ensures fullest enjoyment.

HARRIS OF CALNE

Ready, willing and very able! From the crack of dawn through a long round-and-about day their energy is matched by their fresh-featured ruggedness and handsome style.

THAMES TRUCKS AND VANS BY FORD

CARTOONS

"I managed to get a pair of trousers for you, dear."

"Now let's see—that's twelve quarts of oil at one-and-nine a pint . . ."

"Prefer some of the good ol' slapstick meself."

"For heaven's sake smarten yourself up — have a shave and put a clean apron on."

"I'm always glad when we hear that you're coming—the place gets a good clean up."

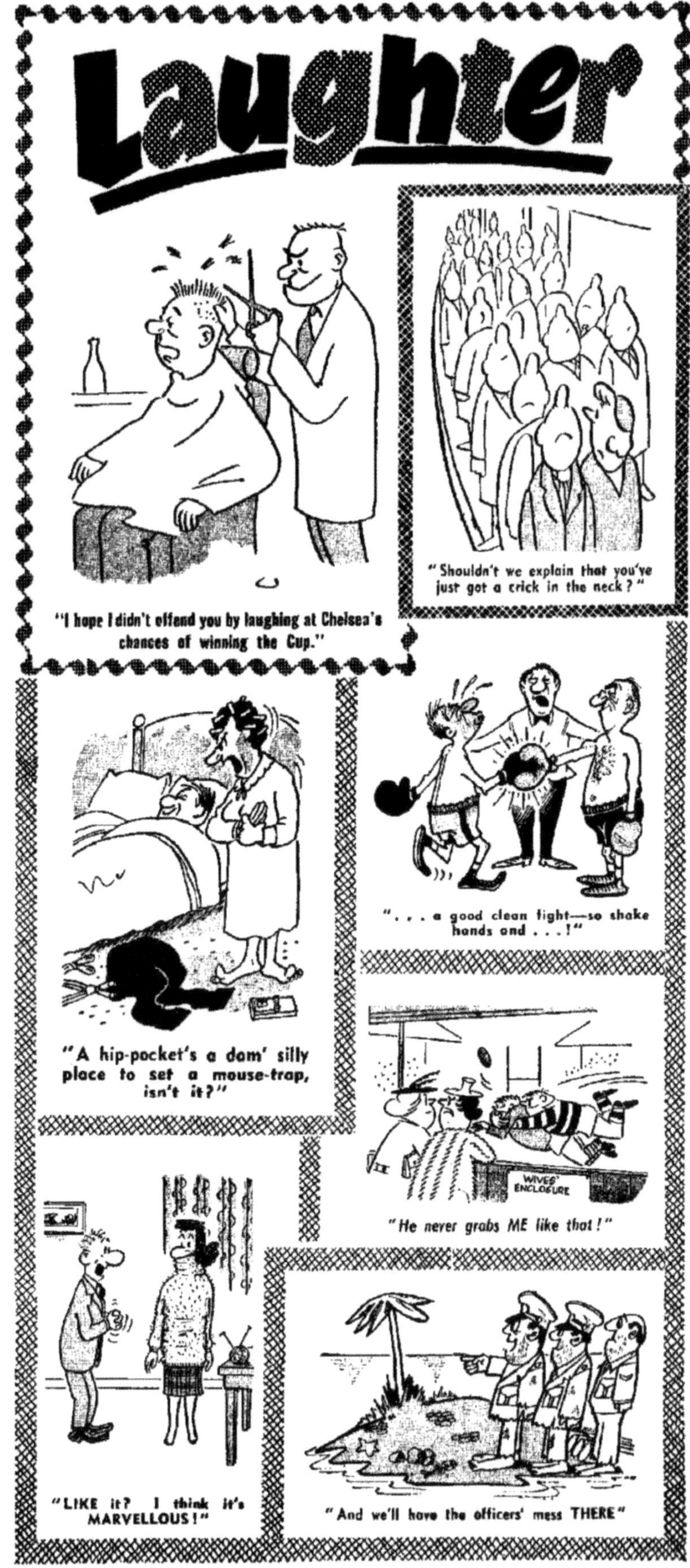
Laughter
"I hope I didn't offend you by laughing at Chelsea's chances of winning the Cup."
"Shouldn't we explain that you've just got a crick in the neck?"
"A hip-pocket's a dam' silly place to set a mouse-trap, isn't it?"
". . . a good clean fight—so shake hands and . . . !"
WIVES' ENCLOSURE
"He never grabs ME like that!"
"LIKE it? I think it's MARVELLOUS!"
"And we'll have the officers' mess THERE"

Printed in Great Britain
by Amazon

41092705R00043